hamlyn
Quick**Cook**

hamlyn
QuickCook
Vegetarian

Recipes by Sunil Vijayakar

Every dish, three ways—you choose!
30 minutes | 20 minutes | 10 minutes

An Hachette UK Company
www.hachette.co.uk

First published in Great Britain in 2012 by Hamlyn,
a division of Octopus Publishing Group Ltd,
Endeavour House, 189 Shaftesbury Avenue,
London, WC2H 8JY, UK
www.octopusbooks.co.uk

Distributed in the US by Hachette Book Group USA
237 Park Avenue, New York, NY 10017 USA
www.octopusbooksusa.com

Distributed in Canada by Canadian Manda Group
165 Dufferin Street, Toronto, Ontario, Canada M6K 3H6

ISBN 978-0-600-62398-4

Printed and bound in China

10 9 8 7 6 5 4 3 2 1

Standard level spoon and cup measurements are used in all recipes unless
otherwise indicated.

Ovens should be preheated to the specified temperature. If using a convection oven,
follow the manufacturer's instructions for adjusting the time and temperature.
Broilers should also be preheated.

This book includes dishes made with nuts and nut derivatives. It is advisable for
those with known allergic reactions to nuts and nut derivatives and those who may
be potentially vulnerable to these allergies, such as pregnant and nursing mothers,
people with a chronic illness, the elderly, babies, and children, to avoid dishes made
with nuts and nut oils.

It is also prudent to check the labels of prepared ingredients for the possible inclusion
of nut derivatives.

The U.S. Department of Agriculture advises that eggs should not be consumed raw.
This book contains some dishes made with raw or lightly cooked eggs. It is prudent
for more vulnerable people, such as pregnant and nursing mothers, those with
weakened immune systems, the elderly, babies, and young children, to avoid dishes
made with raw or lightly cooked eggs.

Contents

Introduction

30 20 10—quick, quicker, quickest

This book offers a new and flexible approach to planning meals for busy cooks and lets you choose the recipe option that best fits the time you have available. Inside you will find 360 dishes that will inspire you and motivate you to cook your own meals every day of the year. All the recipes take a maximum of 30 minutes to cook. Some take as little as 20 minutes and, amazingly, many take only 10 minutes. With a little preparation, you can easily try out one new recipe from this book each night and slowly you will build a wide and exciting portfolio of recipes to suit your needs.

How does it work?

Every recipe in the QuickCook series can be cooked one of three ways—a 30-minute version, a 20-minute version, or a superquick-and-easy 10-minute version. At the beginning of each chapter, you'll find recipes listed by time. Choose a dish based on how much time you have and turn to that page.

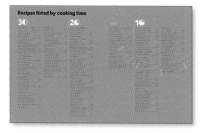

You'll find the main recipe in the middle of the page with a beautiful photograph and two time-variations below.

If you enjoy the dish, you can go back and cook the other time options. If you liked the 20-minute Ravioli with Sweet Potato, Tomatoes, and Arugula (see pages 190–191) but only have 10 minutes on hand, you'll find another way to cook it by using shortcut ingredients or techniques.

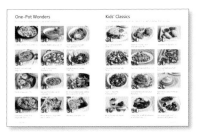

If you love the ingredients and flavors of the 10-minute Asparagus and Udon Noodle Stir-Fry (see pages 218–219), why not try something more substantial, such as the 20-minute Asparagus, Beans, and Udon Noodle Bowl, or be inspired to cook a more elaborate meal using similar ingredients, such as Udon Noodle Pancakes with Grilled Asparagus.

Alternatively, browse through all of the 360 delicious recipes, find something that catches your eye, then cook the version that fits your time frame.

Or, for easy inspiration, turn to the gallery on pages 12–19 to get an instant overview by themes, such as One-Dish Wonders or Kids' Classics.

QuickCook online

And to make life even easier, you can use the special code on each recipe page to email yourself a recipe card for printing, or email a text-only grocery list to your cell. Go to www.hamlynquickcook.com and enter the recipe code at the bottom of each page.

 VEG-SPEC-DOS

QuickCook Vegetarian

A diet rich in fresh vegetables, beans, and whole grains is well documented to be a healthy one. Armed with the knowledge that a diet high in meat protein can be detrimental to health, and with such an abundance of wonderful, seasonal vegetables widely available, it's not difficult to understand why many people choose to follow a vegetarian or "flexitarian" diet.

The key to a well-balanced vegetarian diet is simple: eat plenty of whole grains (brown rice, barley, corn, oats, millet, and buckwheat are all good options), foods that are made from whole grains (such as whole-grain breads, pastas, and cereals), protein-rich beans, lentils, nuts, and eggs, and an abundance of fresh fruit and vegetables. Dairy products (such as butter, cheese, cream, milk, and yogurt) or nondairy alternatives should form a smaller part of the diet and caffeinated drinks, alcohol, and sugary treats should be enjoyed in moderation.

Complex carbohydrates are essential for a good diet and vital for energy. The presence of dietary fiber allows for the energy from the natural sugars they contain to be released slowly, as opposed to refined sugars, which are released into the body quickly and can leave energy levels depleted. Foods rich in complex carbohydrates include those made using the whole of the grain, such as whole-grain bread and whole-wheat pasta, as well as brown rice, barley, corn, buckwheat, dried beans, and bananas.

A healthy vegetarian diet will be high in fiber, which is vital for moving the food in the bowel, helping to prevent intestinal problems and reducing the risk of bowel cancer. Foods rich in fiber can help to lower blood cholesterol, so it is advisable to include high-fiber foods, such as beans and peas, brassica family vegetables (including cabbage, broccoli, and cauliflower) oats, and whole-grain wheat, in most of your meals.

Protein is essential for tissue repair and cell growth and reproduction, especially for growing children and pregnant women. However, we do not need large amounts of protein in our diet and it is perfectly possible to consume the recommended amounts of protein from nonanimal foods. Good sources of vegetarian protein include nuts and seeds, soybean products, peas, beans, chickpeas, and lentils.

QuickCook Techniques and Tips

Creative cookery is not only possible for those who have plenty of time to spend in the kitchen. The recipes in this book can be cooked in a flash using healthy, delicious vegetarian ingredients and with a little help from a well-stocked pantry.

The following pages feature a wide range of quick-to-prepare yet delicious vegetarian dishes, great for those of us who have a busy lifestyle (and who hasn't these days?). These recipes offer the vegetarian cook (or nonvegetarian cook, for that matter) much scope to be inventive in the quickest possible time. Meatless meals need never be boring or bland again.

Using condiments, seasonings, herbs, and spices, can liven up your dining experience, giving you an opportunity to cook and eat a glorious palette of flavors, colors, and textures. Stock up your pantry before you begin to travel through the varied and wonderful world of vegetarian cookery. Most supermarkets will sell everything you'll need, but also try ethnic stores and grocery stores for more unusual ingredients and produce.

A well-equipped kitchen will really help you to save time when preparing your vegetarian meals. A couple of good saucepans of different sizes, a skillet, and a wok are all essentials, and you will find plenty of uses for a good-quality mortar and pestle. A salad spinner speeds up salad washing, and accurately using measuring cups and spoons—making sure dry ingredients are leveled with the straight edge of a knife blade and checking liquid ingredients at eye level—will help to ensure successful results every time. A food processor is a must for quick and easy blending and processing.

QuickCook Ingredients

The secret to being able to cook speedy meals lies in your pantry being well stocked with ingredients that you can use on a day-to-day basis. Once you have a good, varied selection of ingredients in your kitchen, you can choose from a wider selection of recipes to cook at a moment's notice. Remember to check on your stocks regularly and to resupply them when they are running low.

Pantry Staples

It's a good idea to have a variety of dried pasta shapes on hand: linguini, spaghetti, pappardelle, fusilli, penne, and orzo should cover most recipes.

Rice (long-grain, brown, jasmine, and risotto), bulgur wheat, couscous, cornmeal, and quinoa are great basic staples that can be used in a variety of ways to produce wonderful, quick meals.

All-purpose flour is a must for making sauce bases and toppings. Chickpea (besan) flour is great for a spiced batter base to quickly make a variety of crispy vegetable fritters.

Quick-cooking dried beans that don't require long soaking—green or brown lentils, split red lentils, and split peas—are essential for creating delicious vegetarian dishes, and canned beans are handy for instant, last-minute meals. A good supply of kidney beans, chickpeas, black-eyed peas, cannellini beans, and lima beans will really useful.

Healthy, wholesome, and delicious, nuts and seeds will perk up many dishes from salads to stir-fries. Sunflower seeds, sesame seeds, cashew nuts, almonds, pistachios, and walnuts make nutritious additions to vegetarian meals.

Packed with flavor and color, canned tomatoes and tomato puree have a multitude of uses and are a terrific standby for making quick sauces, casseroles, and stews.

Good-quality olive oil, sunflower oil, vegetable oil, and toasted sesame seed oil are great for stir-frying and general-purpose cooking. Red wine vinegar, white wine vinegar, balsamic vinegar, cider vinegar, and rice wine vinegar are a must for creating quick salad dressings and sauces.

Flavorings

You cannot have enough of a variety of dried herbs and spices in your pantry to experiment with flavors. The list is endless, but always remember to buy them in small quantities and use within three months for maximum flavor. A good stock of dried herbs (basil, thyme, oregano, tarragon, rosemary, and parsley are a good starting point), whole spices (cumin seeds, coriander seeds, black mustard seeds, cloves, cardamom pods, and cinnamon sticks) and ground spices (cumin, cinnamon, coriander, chili powder, paprika, and turmeric) will really add depth to your dishes. Sea salt and fresh black peppercorns are also a must.

Stock up on a selection of sauces and condiments to add instant flavor to your dishes. Soy sauce, sweet chili sauce, Tabasco sauce, and Worcestershire sauce are staples you will use time and time again. Honey and maple syrup are good sweeteners to keep on hand for both sweet and savory recipes.

Fresh Food

Keeping your refrigerator well stocked will enable you to put together healthy and tasty vegetarian meals in minutes. The key is to buy fresh produce regularly, and to only buy what you know you will use to minimize wastage. Fresh pasta, tofu, cheese, butter, milk, cream, and eggs are always great to have in the refrigerator. You'll also find lemons, limes, red chiles, fresh ginger, scallions, and fresh herbs are great additions to speedy meals.

Buy fruit and vegetables that are in season and, if possible, locally grown. The goodness and flavor will be far superior to those that have been grown out of season or have traveled many miles to reach the supermarket shelves. Garlic, onions, potatoes, shallots, carrots, and other root vegetables and most types of fruit will keep well for a few days in the pantry.

Cheesy Treats

The ultimate comfort food, these cheese-based dishes will satisfy and delight.

Baked Goat Cheese with Honey and Pistachio 24

Camembert "Fondue" with Honey and Walnuts 36

Hot-Crumbed Bocconcini with Fresh Pesto and Aioli 52

Spiced Paneer Bruschettas 56

Watermelon, Olive, Green Bean, and Feta Salad 100

Broiled Haloumi, Bell Pepper, and Arugula Salad 116

Cauliflower and Cheese 156

Smoked Cheese, Roasted Pepper, and Spinach Quesadillas 164

Asparagus and Fontina Cheese Crespelles 180

Tarragon and Cheddar Cheese Soufflé Omelet 188

Deep-Fried Haloumi Beer-Battered Fritters 192

Broccoli and Blue Cheese Soufflés 210

Pasta and Noodles

Hearty and healthy, pasta and noodles are the ultimate fast food.

Warm Pasta Salad with
Lemon and Broccoli 94

Delicatessen Pasta Salad 102

Creamy Zucchini
Orzo Pasta 128

Spinach, Cherry Tomato, and
Blue Cheese Pasta Salad 140

Kale and Pecorino
Pesto Linguini 144

Pasta with Asparagus, Beans,
and Pesto 148

Rigatoni with Fresh Tomato,
Chile, Garlic, and Basil 152

Tomato and Eggplant
Pappardelle 160

Cold Asian Summer
Soba Noodle Salad 168

Tortellini, Roasted Pepper,
and Arugula Salad 170

Tagliatelle with Squash
and Sage 184

Ravioli with Sweet Potato,
Tomatoes, and Arugula 190

One-Dish Wonders

When time is short, these one-dish meals will save the day.

Spinach and Potato Tortilla 50

Chunky Mushroom Soup 74

Asian Rice Soup with
Egg and Greens 84

Spinach and Red Lentil
Soup 86

Greek-Style
Summer Omelet 130

Mixed Bean and Tomato
Chili 146

Ranch-Style Eggs 150

Spinach with Cherry
Tomatoes 154

Broccoli and Mushrooms in Black
Bean Sauce with Noodles 182

Malaysian Coconut and
Vegetable Stew 194

Lima Bean and Vegetable
Nut Casserole 222

Blackberry Crisp 236

Kids' Classics

Please the little people in your life with these fruit- and vegetable-filled favorites.

**Corn and Bean
Tortilla Stack** 40

**Corn Cakes with
Avocado Salsa** 46

Vegetable Spring Rolls 62

**Quick Roasted Vegetable
Pizzas** 124

Stir-Fried Vegetable Rice 158

**Pesto and Antipasti
Puff Tart** 198

**Flash-In-The-Pan
Ratatouille** 200

**Scallion, Dill, and Chive
Pancakes** 212

**Quick Mini Lemon
Meringue Pies** 230

**Berry, Honey, and Yogurt
Desserts** 234

**French Toast with
Mixed Berries** 246

**Chocolate Fondue with a
Selection of Dippers** 258

Spicy Specials

These tasty dishes will really pack a punch at mealtimes.

Grilled Corn Cobettes with Herb and Chile Butter 26

Bulgur Wheat Salad with Roasted Peppers on Lettuce 30

Spiced Onion Fritters with Mint and Cilantro Relish 38

Chile, Tomato, and Cannellini Beans on Bruschetta 42

Spiced Potato, Cilantro, and Celeriac Soup 70

Jamaican Spiced Corn Chowder 82

Tex-Mex Corn Salad 162

Vegetable Pad Thai 186

Nasi Goreng 196

Spicy Szechuan Tofu and Vegetable Stir-Fry 204

Quick Curried Egg Salad 224

Spiced Caramelized Pineapple with Rum 260

Fruity Favorites

Packed with nutritious fruit, here are some delicious ways to your five a day.

Endive Boats with Gorgonzola, Pear, and Walnuts 28

Beet and Apple Soup 72

Fruity Potato Salad 106

Couscous Salad with Bell Peppers and Preserved Lemon 110

Quinoa, Zucchini, and Pomegranate Salad 118

Jeweled Fruity Spicy Pilaf 178

Lemon and Herb Risotto 216

Baked Amaretto Figs 232

Instant Mixed Berry Sorbet 248

Peach and Raspberry Cheesecake Desserts 254

Watermelon, Lime, and Grenadine Squares 268

Lime, Banana, and Coconut Fritters 274

Spring Selection

Make the most of everything the season has to offer with these fabulous recipes.

Deluxe Eggs Florentine 32

Lettuce, Pea, and Tarragon Soup 76

Iced Green Gazpacho 80

Veggie Caesar-Style Salad with Garlic and Herb Croutons 92

Cucumber and Basmati Rice Salad 108

Green Vegetable Curry 134

Rustic Italian-Style Mushrooms with Cornmeal 136

Creamy Mushroom and Herb Pancakes 172

Roasted Vegetable Couscous Salad 202

Berries with Meringue 252

Rhubarb, Orange, and Ginger Desserts 256

Strawberry and Cream Layer Cake 264

Fall Delights

The perfect dishes to brighten up cool days in the fall.

Stuffed Eggplant and Yogurt Rolls 34

Creamy Tarragon Mushrooms on Brioche Toast 44

Hearty Minestrone 78

Moroccan Bulgur Wheat and Roasted Vegetable Salad 96

Black-Eyed Pea and Red Pepper "Stew" 126

Beet Pasta with Herbs 132

Herby Bulgur Wheat and Chickpea Salad 166

Moroccan Vegetable Tagine 206

Eggplant and Harissa Sauté 208

Cherry and Vanilla Brûlée 238

Molten Chocolate Lava Cakes 240

Spiced Pancakes with Ice Cream and Chocolate Sauce 242

QuickCook

Snacks and Light Bites

Recipes listed by cooking time

30 Baked Goat Cheese with Honey and Pistachio

Serves 4

8 grape vine leaves, rinsed well
  in cold water
melted butter, for brushing
½ cup pistachio nuts
4 small Crottin de Chèvre or
  other small, round goat cheeses
4 teaspoons white wine

For the salad

1 garlic clove, crushed
2 tablespoons cider vinegar
1 tablespoon honey
⅓ cup extra virgin olive oil
2 pears, cored and thinly sliced
2 small radicchio, leaves separated
salt and pepper

- Gently dry the grape vine leaves, then on a clean surface lay one flat and partly overlap another leaf side by side (by about one-third). Repeat with the other 6 vine leaves; you should end up with 4 pairs. Brush the leaves with a little melted butter and set aside. Process the pistachio nuts in a small food processor until coarsely ground.

- Brush the cheeses with the remaining melted butter and then roll them in the chopped pistachios to coat. Place a cheese portion in the center of each pair of leaves and sprinkle with the wine. Form a package by bringing the leaves up around each cheese and secure with string or toothpicks. Place the cheese packages on a baking sheet and bake in a preheated oven, at 325°F, for 12–15 minutes.

- Meanwhile, make the salad. Whisk the garlic, vinegar, honey, and seasoning together, then gradually whisk in the oil. Toss with the pear and radicchio leaves and set aside.

- Serve the crottins, still in their grape vine leaf wrappings to be unwrapped at the table, accompanied by the salad.

---

10 Goat Cheese, Pear, and Pistachio Melts

Rub 4 slices sourdough bread with 2 halved garlic cloves and drizzle each with 1 tablespoon olive oil. Thinly slice 1 pear and arrange over the bread. Sprinkle with 1 cup chopped pistachio nuts and cover with thin slices from 2 small Crottin de Chèvre or other goat cheese. Cook under a preheated hot broiler for 2–3 minutes, until the cheese is just melting and serve with a radicchio salad.

20 Broiled Goat Cheese, Pear, Radicchio, and Pistachio Salad

Thickly slice a 10 oz log goat cheese. Toss 1 head radicchio leaves in 1 tablespoon olive oil and season. Slice 2 pears and arrange with the radicchio on 4 serving plates. Transfer the goat cheese slices to a sheet of aluminum foil and cook under a preheated medium broiler for 2 minutes, or until just melted. Divide among the 4 plates, drizzle with ¼ cup olive oil and 2 tablespoons cider vinegar. To finish, scatter 1 cup chopped pistachio nuts over the top and drizzle with 1 tablespoon honey. Serve immediately.

Grilled Corn Cobettes with Herb and Chile Butter

Serves 4

4 ears of corn, husks removed

For the herb and chile butter

½ lb (2 sticks) butter, softened
⅓ cup finely chopped dill
2 red chiles, seeded and
  finely chopped

- Mix together all the ingredients for the herb and chile butter and set aside.

- Cut each corn cob into 3 equal pieces or cobettes. Insert a presoaked wooden or a metal skewer into the side of each cobette and place on a barbecue or hot ridged grill pan and cook, turning frequently, for 4–5 minutes or until lightly charred and blistered in places.

- Remove the cobettes from the heat, brush with the butter, and serve immediately.

Speedy Spicy Corn Chowder

Add 2½ cups fresh corn kernels to a saucepan with 4 sliced scallions, 1 seeded and finely chopped red chile, 1¼ cups heavy cream, and 2 cups vegetable stock. Bring to a boil, stir in 2 tablespoons chopped cilantro, and serve immediately.

Corn and Herb Frittata

Lightly beat 6 eggs in a bowl, season with salt and pepper, and add 2 tablespoons each of chopped cilantro, dill, and mint. Heat 2 tablespoons olive oil in medium, nonstick skillet and add ½ small chopped onion, 1 seeded and finely chopped red chile, and 2 crushed garlic cloves. Stir-fry for 3–4 minutes and then toss in 2½ cups fresh corn kernels and stir-fry for another 2–3 minutes. Pour the egg mixture over the top and cook on medium heat for 10 minutes or until the bottom is set. Place the skillet under a preheated medium broiler for 4–5 minutes or until the top is set and golden. Remove from the heat, cut into wedges, and serve.

Endive Boats with Gorgonzola, Pear, and Walnuts

Serves 4

1 ripe pear, cored and finely
chopped
2 tablespoons crème fraîche
or sour cream
½ cup crumbled Gorgonzola
cheese or other blue cheese
20 Belgian endive leaves,
raddichio leaves, or a mixture
of both
¼ cup coarsely chopped walnuts,
toasted
olive oil, to drizzle

- Mix together the pear, crème fraîche, and Gorgonzola in a small bowl.

- Arrange the endive leaves on a serving platter and spoon a little of the pear mixture onto the bottom end of each leaf.

- Sprinkle the chopped nuts over the top of the filling, drizzle with a little olive oil, and serve.

Braised Endive and Beans with Gorgonzola Cut 4 heads Belgian endive lengthwise into quarters, but do not trim off the end. Melt ¼ pound (1 stick) butter in a large skillet, add the endive, and cook for 4–5 minutes, turning occasionally, until golden. Add 2 thinly sliced leeks, 1 (15 oz) can lima beans, drained, 1 cup hot vegetable stock, 2 teaspoons sugar, 1 cup crumbled Gorgonzola cheese or other blue cheese, and ¼ cup crème fraîche or sour cream. Bring to a boil, cover, and simmer for 6–8 minutes. Turn the endive over, increase the heat, and cook for another 1–2 minutes, until the leeks are tender and the gravy has thickened. Serve immediately with crusty bread.

Baked Radicchio and Gorgonzola Trim any coarse or bruised outer leaves from 8 large heads raddichio. Place in an ovenproof dish into which they will fit snugly in a single layer. Drizzle ⅓ cup olive oil over the top and season to taste. Scatter with 1 cup crumbled Gorgonzola cheese or other blue cheese and the juice of 1 lemon. Bake in a preheated oven, at 350°F, for 20 minutes. Serve straight from the ovenproof dish with the juices and scatter with ¼ cup chopped toasted walnuts before serving.

Bulgur Wheat Salad with Roasted Peppers on Lettuce

Serves 4

1⅓ cups bulgur wheat
1 tablespoon tomato paste
juice of 1½ lemons
⅓ cup extra virgin olive oil
1 red chile, finely chopped
1 cup drained and diced roasted
   red peppers (from a jar)
8 scallions, finely sliced
1¾ cup diced tomatoes
1 cup coarsely chopped
   flat leaf parsley
½ cup coarsely chopped mint
4 Boston lettuce, leaves
   separated
salt

- Put the bulgur wheat in a bowl, pour ½ cup boiling water over the grains, stir, cover, and let stand for 10–15 minutes, until the grains are tender.

- Add the tomato paste, lemon juice, olive oil, red chile, and some salt to the bulgur wheat mixture and mix thoroughly.

- Add the roasted red peppers, scallions, and tomatoes, together with the parsley and mint, and mix well.

- Arrange the lettuce leaves around the edges of a serving plate with the bulgur salad in the center. Use the leaves to scoop up the bulgur mixture and eat.

1 **Roasted Red Pepper, Marinated Vegetable, and Bulgur Wheat Salad** Prepare the bulgur wheat mixture as above and place in a salad bowl. Add 1 cup of drained, marinated mixed vegetables that includes roasted red peppers to the bulgur wheat. Finish off with 1 chopped red chile and ¼ cup chopped flat leaf parsley, toss to mix well, and serve.

2 **Layered Roasted Red Pepper, Bulgur Wheat, and Tomatoes** Prepare the bulgur wheat mixture as above and put into medium, shallow ovenproof dish with 1 cup drained and diced roasted red pepper (from a jar). Slice 4 plum tomatoes and place over the bulgur wheat to cover. Sprinkle with 1 finely chopped red chile and drizzle ¼ cup olive oil over the top. Cook under a preheated medium broiler for

5 minutes. Crumble 1 cup feta cheese on top and scatter with 8 chopped, pitted ripe black olives. Return the dish to the broiler for 4–5 minutes or until the feta is browned. Serve immediately.

Deluxe Eggs Florentine

Serves 4

12 asparagus spears, trimmed

2 tablespoons butter, plus extra for buttering

5 cups baby spinach

pinch of freshly grated nutmeg

2 English muffins, halved and lightly toasted

1 tablespoon vinegar

4 extra-large eggs

½ cup store-bought hollandaise sauce, to serve

salt and pepper

- Blanch the asparagus spears in a saucepan of boiling water for 2–3 minutes, drain, and keep warm.

- Meanwhile, melt the butter in a large skillet, add the spinach, and stir-fry for 3 minutes or until just wilted. Season with grated nutmeg, salt, and black pepper.

- Split and toast the muffins, and butter them just before serving.

- Poach the eggs by bringing a saucepan of lightly salted water to a boil. Add the vinegar and reduce to a gentle simmer. Swirl the water with a fork and crack 2 of the eggs into the water. Cook for 3–4 minutes, remove carefully with a slotted spoon, and repeat with the remaining 2 eggs.

- Meanwhile, heat the hollandaise sauce according to the package directions.

- Top the toasted muffins with some spinach and a poached egg and spoon the hollandaise over the egg. Sprinkle with freshly ground black pepper and serve each egg with 3 asparagus spears on the side.

Warm Asparagus Salad with Sunny-Side-Up Eggs Cook 1 lb asparagus, trimmed, in a saucepan of lightly salted, boiling water for 4–5 minutes. Drain and place in a wide bowl with ¼ cup olive oil, season, and toss to mix well. Meanwhile, fry 4 eggs in a large nonstick skillet for 2–3 minutes. Divide the asparagus among 4 warm plates, sprinkle 1 tablespoon grated Parmesan over each serving, and top with a fried egg. Serve immediately.

Spinach, Asparagus, and Egg Tortilla Beat together 6 eggs with 12 torn basil leaves and season well. Heat 2 tablespoons olive oil in a large skillet and add the egg mixture. Coarsely chopped a large handful of baby spinach leaves, 12 asparagus spears, and 1 tomato. Scatter the spinach, asparagus and tomatoes evenly over the egg. Cook the tortilla for about 6–8 minutes without stirring and then place under a preheated medium broiler for 3–4 minutes or until golden brown all over. Cut the tortilla into wedges and serve with a green salad.

Stuffed Eggplant and Yogurt Rolls

Serves 4

1 garlic clove, crushed

3 tablespoons Greek yogurt

1⅓ cups crumbled feta cheese

⅓ cup finely chopped oregano

2 eggplants

olive oil, for brushing and drizzling

1 cup sun-dried tomatoes, soaked in water for 1–2 hours

a handful basil leaves

salt and pepper

· In a bowl combine the garlic, yogurt, feta, and oregano. Stir well, season to taste, and set aside.

· Meanwhile slice the eggplants into slices ¼ inch thick. Put a heavy, ridged grill pan over high heat, brush the eggplant slices with a little oil, and grill, in batches, until they begin to char and soften.

· Spread each eggplant slice with the yogurt mixture and top with a basil leaf and a sun-dried tomato. Roll the slices up, garnish with basil leaves, drizzle a little olive oil over the top, and serve.

1⃝ Stuffed Zucchini Rolls

Replace the eggplants with 2 large zucchini and grill as in the recipe above. Replace the oregano with chopped mint leaves and the sun-dried tomatoes with ¼ cup thinly sliced roasted red peppers (from a jar), and garnish with mint leaves.

2⃝ Eggplant, Feta, and Couscous

Salad Grill the eggplants as in the recipe above. Meanwhile, place ¾ cup couscous in a bowl and just cover with boiling water. Cover and let stand for 10 minutes or until the liquid is completely absorbed. Cut the eggplant into bite-size pieces and place in a salad bowl with the couscous, 1 cup sun-dried tomatoes, a small handful of basil leaves, and 1⅓ cups cubed feta cheese. Drizzle 3 tablespoons of olive oil over the top and serve at room temperature.

Camembert "Fondue" with Honey and Walnuts

Serves 4

1 small Camembert cheese, in a lidded box

6 walnut halves, coarsely chopped

2 tablespoons thyme leaves, plus extra time sprigs, to garnish

2 tablespoons honey

crusty bread and vegetable sticks, such as carrots and celery, to serve

- Remove the cheese from its box and discard any paper or plastic wrapping. Slice off the top rind and replace the cheese in its box.

- Sprinkle the walnuts and thyme over the top of the cheese, and drizzle with the honey.

- Replace the lid and place the box in the center of a preheated oven, at 425°F, for 5–10 minutes. Depending on the ripeness of the cheese, it should be runny inside when cooked.

- Garnish with thyme sprigs and serve warm with crusty bread and vegetable sticks.

Camembert, Walnut, and Broiled Tomato Open Sandwich

Lightly toast 4 large slices sourdough bread and spread each with a teaspoon Dijon mustard. Slice 2 plum tomatoes and lay on top of the mustard. Place 2 slices Camembert cheese over each piece of toast and place under a preheated medium broiler for 2–3 minutes or until bubbling. Scatter 2 tablespoons chopped walnuts over the top and serve immediately with a salad.

Camembert and Walnut Pasta

Cook 12 oz penne according to the package directions. Drain and keep warm. Meanwhile, finely slice 2 garlic cloves and 4 scallions and stir-fry in a tablespoon olive oil in a large skillet for 1–2 minutes. Add 2 chopped tomatoes and stir-fry for 5–6 minutes over medium heat. Finely chop 2 tablespoons tarragon and add to the tomato mixture. Add the drained pasta to the skillet with 7 oz chopped Camembert cheese and 1 cup chopped walnuts, toasted, and stir to mix well. Season and serve ladled into warm bowls.

30 Spiced Onion Fritters with Mint and Cilantro Relish

Serves 4

3–4 onions, sliced
1 teaspoon red chili powder
1 teaspoon ground turmeric
2 teaspoons cumin seeds
1 tablespoon coriander seeds, crushed
2¾ cups chickpea (besan) flour
vegetable oil, for deep-frying
sea salt

For the relish

½ cup finely chopped mint
⅓ cup finely chopped cilantro
1 cup plain yogurt, whisked
1 tablespoon lime juice
1 tablespoon mint jelly

- First make the relish by mixing all the ingredients together in a bowl, season well, and chill until ready to serve.

- Separate the sliced onions in a large bowl. Add the chili powder, turmeric, cumin seeds, and crushed coriander seeds, and season with sea salt. Mix well. Add the chickpea flour a little at a time, stirring again to coat the onions. Now gradually sprinkle some cold water over this mixture, adding just enough water to make a sticky batter that coats the onions. Use your fingers to mix thoroughly.

- Fill a deep, wide saucepan one-quarter full with vegetable oil and place over high heat until it reaches 350°F or a cube of bread sizzles and turns golden in 10–15 seconds.

- Drop spoonfuls of the mixture into the oil. Fry in batches over medium-high heat for 1–2 minutes or until golden brown and crisp on the outside. Remove with a slotted spoon and drain on paper towels. Serve immediately with the relish.

10 Spiced Fried Okra

Place ¾ cup chickpea (besan) flour in a bowl. Slice 12 oz okra lengthwise into quarters and toss in the flour. Pour vegetable oil into a large saucepan to a depth of 1 inch and heat until a bread crumb sizzles gently when placed in the oil. Fry the okra until crisp and golden brown, stirring ccasionally. Remove with a slotted spoon and transfer to a bowl lined with paper towels. Sprinkle 1 teaspoon each of salt, chili powder, and dried mango powder over them and toss well. Serve hot with naan.

20 Spiced Chickpea Flour Pancakes

Put 1⅔ cups chickpea (besan) flour into a mixing bowl. Slowly add 2 cups water, mixing to a smooth batter. Add ½ teaspoon each of salt, cayenne pepper, and cumin seeds, 1 finely chopped red onion, 1 teaspoon grated ginger, 4 finely chopped green chiles, 4 chopped garlic cloves, and 2 tablespoons chopped cilantro. Smear a large nonstick skillet with 1 teaspoon vegetable oil, using paper towels, and set over medium heat. When hot, stir the batter and pour about ¼ cup into the center of the skillet. Quickly tilt the skillet in all directions, spreading the batter to make a 7–7½ inch diameter pancake. Cover and cook for 3 minutes or until the pancake is reddish brown at the bottom. Dribble another teaspoon of oil around the edges of the pancake. Turn it over and cook, uncovered, for another minute or until golden. Remove from the heat and cover with a plate. Repeat with the remaining batter to make 8 pancakes. Serve immediately with yogurt and mango chutney.

Corn and Bean Tortilla Stack

Serves 4

2 red bell peppers, seeded
   and chopped
2 tablespoons olive oil
1 (14½ oz) can chopped tomatoes
2 (15 oz) cans kidney beans,
   drained
1 (15¼ oz) can corn kernels,
   drained
½ teaspoon chili powder
4 large corn tortillas
1¾ cups shredded cheddar cheese
1 tablespoon finely chopped
   cilantro, to garnish

To serve

sour cream (optional)
1 avocado, peeled, pitted,
   and sliced (optional)

- Place the chopped bell peppers and olive oil in a large saucepan, cover, and cook gently for 5 minutes. Add the tomatoes, beans, corn kernels, and chili powder. Bring to a boil and simmer, uncovered, for 7–8 minutes, until the mixture is thick.

- Place 1 tortilla on a baking sheet. Top with one-third of the bean mixture and one-quarter of the cheese. Repeat this twice to make 3 layers, then place the final tortilla on top. Sprinkle with the remaining cheese and bake in a preheated oven, at 375°F, for 15 minutes.

- Garnish with the chopped cilantro and serve with avocado and sour cream, if desired.

Bean and Corn Wraps

Spread 4 corn tortillas with 2 tablespoons mayonnaise each. Mix together 1 (8¾ oz) can corn kernels and ½ cup of canned kidney beans. Divide this mixture among the tortillas and sprinkle each with a tablespoon shredded cheddar cheese. Roll up the tortillas to encase the filling and serve.

Spicy Tortilla Chips with a Creamy Bean Dip

Take 4 corn tortillas and cut each one into 12 wedges. Place on a large baking sheet and drizzle with a little olive oil and sprinkle with 2 teaspoons cumin seeds and 2 teaspoons smoked paprika. Bake in a preheated oven, at 350°F, for 8–10 minutes or until crisp. Meanwhile make the dip.

Drain and rinse the beans from 2 (15 oz) cans kidney beans and transfer to a food processor along with 2 crushed garlic cloves, ⅓ cup finely chopped parsley, and 1 cup cream cheese with garlic and herbs, then blend until smooth. Season and serve with the tortilla chips.

Chile, Tomato, and Cannellini Beans on Bruschetta

Serves 4

3 tablespoons extra virgin olive oil, plus extra for drizzling

2 teaspoons chopped rosemary

1 red chile, chopped

2 (15 oz) cans cannellini beans, drained

2 tablespoons chopped sun-dried tomatoes, soaked in water for 1–2 hours

8 slices day-old bread from a sourdough loaf

2 garlic cloves, halved

sea salt and pepper

To garnish

basil

lemon wedges

- Heat the oil in a skillet over low heat. Add the rosemary and chile and cook for a few seconds, until the mixture starts to sizzle. Add the beans and stir-fry for 2–3 minutes.

- Transfer to a food processor and process until coarsely combined. Season to taste with sea salt and pepper and fold in the chopped tomatoes.

- Heat a heavy, ridged grill pan and warm the bread slices over medium-high heat until lightly charred, or toast in a toaster. Rub the warm bread with the garlic halves and drizzle generously with olive oil. Sprinkle lightly with sea salt and top with the bean mixture.

- Sprinkle with freshly ground black pepper and lightly drizzle again with oil. Garnish with basil and lemon wedges.

Spicy Tomato and Bean Soup

Heat 3 cups of canned tomato soup and stir in 1 finely chopped red chile and 1 (15 oz) can cannellini beans, drained and rinsed. Bring to a boil and serve piping hot with toasted sourdough bread.

Vegetable and Cannellini Bean Gratin

Cook a 1 lb package prepared vegetables (such as broccoli florets, cauliflower, and carrots) in a large saucepan of boiling water for 3–4 minutes. Drain and transfer to a shallow ovenproof dish and mix with 1 (14 oz) jar tomato pasta sauce and 1 (15 oz) can cannellini beans, drained and rinsed. Mix together 4 cups fresh bread crumbs with 1 cup grated Parmesan cheese and sprinkle over the vegetable mixture. Bake in a preheated oven, at 400°F, for 15–20 minutes, until bubbling and golden. Serve immediately.

Creamy Tarragon Mushrooms on Brioche Toasts

Serves 4

8 slices brioche
¼ lb plus 2 tablespoons (1¼ sticks) butter
2 shallots, finely chopped
3 garlic cloves, finely chopped
1 red chile, seeded and finely chopped (optional)
10 oz mixed wild mushrooms (such as chanterelle, porcini, and oyster), trimmed and sliced
¼ cup crème fraîche or sour cream, plus extra to garnish (optional)
2 tablespoons finely chopped tarragon
1 tablespoon finely chopped flat leaf parsley
salt and pepper

- Lightly toast the brioche slices and keep warm.

- Heat the butter in a skillet and sauté the shallots, garlic, and chile, if using, for 1–2 minutes. Now add the mushrooms and stir-fry over medium heat for 6–8 minutes. Season well, remove from the heat, and stir in the crème fraîche and chopped herbs.

- Spoon the mushrooms onto the sliced brioche and serve immediately, with an extra dollop of crème fraîche, if desired.

Chunky Mushroom and Tarragon Soup

Heat 3 cups of canned cream of mushroom soup in a saucepan along with 2 (8 oz) cans whole button mushrooms. Bring to a boil and simmer for 2–3 minutes until piping hot. Stir in ½ cup chopped tarragon and serve immediately, garnished with a little chopped flat leaf parsley.

Mushroom and Tarragon Risotto

Bring 5 cups vegetable stock to a boil and keep hot. Meanwhile, heat 2 tablespoons olive oil in a large, heavy saucepan and add 1 chopped onion and 2 chopped garlic cloves. Cook over low heat for 2–3 minutes, until softened. Add 8 oz mixed wild mushrooms (as above) and cook for another 2–3 minutes, until browned. Stir in 2 cups risotto rice and stir to coat with the oil. Pour in ⅔ cup dry white wine and simmer, stirring, until the liquid has been absorbed. Add a ladleful of the hot stock and simmer, stirring again, until the liquid has been absorbed. Continue adding the stock in this way, until all the liquid has been absorbed and the rice is plump and tender. Finish by stirring in 2 tablespoons each of chopped tarragon and parsley, and 3 tablespoons butter. Season well and serve with freshly grated Parmesan.

Corn Cakes with Avocado Salsa

Serves 4

3½ cups fresh corn kernels
4 scallions, finely sliced
2 eggs
⅓ cup finely chopped cilantro,
  plus extra to garnish
1 cup all-purpose flour
1 teaspoon baking powder
salt and pepper
vegetable oil, for frying

For the avocado salsa

2 ripe avocados, peeled,
  pitted, and finely diced
¼ cup each of chopped
  mint and cilantro
2 tablespoons lime juice
2 tablespoons finely chopped
  red onion
½ teaspoon Tabasco sauce

- Place three-quarters of the corn kernels along with the scallions, eggs, cilantro, flour, and baking powder in a food processor and process until combined. Season well and transfer to a large bowl. Add the remaining corn kernels and mix well.

- Heat 1 tablespoon of vegetable oil in a large nonstick skillet over medium-high heat. When the oil is hot, drop heaping tablespoons of the mixture into the skillet and cook in batches for 1 minute on each side.

- Drain the corn cakes on paper towels and keep warm in a preheated oven, at 250°F, while making the rest of the cakes.

- To make the avocado salsa, place all the ingredients in a bowl and stir gently to combine.

- Serve the warm corn cakes accompanied by the tangy avocado salsa and garnished with cilantro.

---

1 Corn, Arugula, and Avocado Salad

Cut each corn cake into quarters and place in a salad bowl with the avocado salsa. Stir in 4½ cups arugula and drizzle with ¼ cup olive oil. Toss gently to mix well and serve.

2 Pea and Mint Fritters

Replace the corn in the recipe above with thawed frozen peas and the cilantro with chopped mint and proceed as above. Stir ⅓ cup plain yogurt into the salsa and serve with the pea and mint fritters.

Greek Salad with Toasted Pita Breads

Serves 4

4 oz feta cheese, crumbled into smallish chunks

8–10 fresh mint leaves, shredded

1 cup pitted kalamata olives

2 tomatoes, chopped

juice of a large lemon

1 small red onion, thinly sliced

1 teaspoon dried oregano

4 pita breads

lemon wedges, to serve

· In a bowl, toss together the feta, mint, olives, tomatoes, lemon juice, onion and oregano.

· Toast the pitas under a preheated hot grill until lightly golden, then split open and toast the open sides.

· Tear the hot pitas into bite-size pieces, then toss with the other ingredients in the bowl. Serve with lemon wedges.

2 **Broiled Feta, Spinach, and Pine Nut Salad** Place an 8 oz block feta cheese on a baking sheet and sprinkle with 1 teaspoon dried oregano. Place under a preheated hot broiler for 5–6 minutes or until lightly browned. Meanwhile put 10 oz baby spinach in a wide bowl with 1 sliced red onion, 2 chopped tomatoes, and ¼ cup toasted pine nuts. Sprinkle with 2 tablespoons sherry vinegar, then drizzle with ⅓ cup olive oil. Season well and toss. Cut the broiled feta into small cubes, scatter over the salad, and serve.

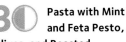

3 **Pasta with Mint and Feta Pesto, Olives, and Roasted Vegetables** Place 1 red and 1 yellow bell pepper, seeded and cut into 1 inch pieces, 1 medium eggplant, cut into 1 inch pieces, 1 zucchini, cut into 1 inch cubes, and 2 small red onions, peeled and cut into wedges, on a large nonstick baking sheet. Drizzle with a little olive oil and season well. Roast in a preheated oven, at 400°F, for 15–20 minutes, or until the edges of the vegetables are just starting to char. Meanwhile, bring a large saucepan of salted water to a boil. Cook 12 oz rigatoni in the water, according to the package directions. Toast ¾ cup pine nuts in a dry skillet for 4–5 minutes, until golden brown, stirring often to prevent them from burning. Transfer to a food processor with 1 cup olive oil, 4 chopped garlic cloves, ½ cup each of chopped mint and basil leaves, and 1 cup crumbled feta to make a coarse pesto. Check the seasoning. Drain the cooked pasta, return to the pan with the roasted vegetables and 1 cup pitted kalamata olives, and stir in the pesto. Serve immediately.

Spinach and Potato Tortilla

Serves 4

3 tablespoons olive oil

2 onions, finely chopped

1¼ cups peeled and cubed
cooked potatoes

2 garlic cloves, finely chopped

1 cup coasely chopped,
thoroughly drained,
cooked spinach
coarsely chopped

¼ cup finely chopped
roasted red pepper

5 eggs, lightly beaten

3–4 tablespoons grated
Manchego cheese

salt and pepper

- Heat the oil in a nonstick skillet and add the onions and potatoes. Cook gently over medium heat for 3–4 minutes or until the vegetables have softened but not colored, turning and stirring often.

- Add the garlic, spinach, and red pepper and stir to mix well.

- Beat the eggs lightly and season well. Pour into the skillet, shaking the pan so that the egg is evenly spread. Cook gently for 8–10 minutes or until the tortilla is set at the bottom.

- Sprinkle over the grated Manchego. Place the skillet under a preheated medium-hot broiler and cook for 3–4 minutes or until the top is set and golden.

- Remove from the heat, cut into bite-size squares or triangles and serve warm or at room temperature.

1 Spinach and Potato Sauté

Heat 1 tablespoon vegetable oil in a large skillet. Add 2 chopped garlic cloves, 1 finely chopped onion, and 1 tablespoon curry powder. Stir in ½ cup tomato puree, 1 (10 oz) package baby leaf spinach, and 1 cup cooked, cubed potatoes. Sauté over high heat for 2–3 minutes or until piping hot. Season and serve with crusty bread or rice.

2 Spanish and Potato Stew

Heat 2 tablespoons olive oil in a saucepan and add 4 crushed garlic cloves, 1 chopped onion, 1 finely chopped red bell pepper, 1 lb fresh spinach leaves, chopped, and 2 medium potatoes cut into ½ inch cubes. Add 4 cups hot vegetable stock and a pinch of saffron threads. Bring to a boil and cook for 12–15 minutes or until the potatoes are tender. Season and serve with crusty bread or rice.

Hot-Crumbed Bocconcini with Fresh Pesto Aioli

Serves 4

2 cups fresh white bread crumbs
zest of 1 lemon, finely grated
generous pinch of crushed
   red pepper
2 tablespoons fresh thyme
⅓ cup all-purpose flour
2 extra-large eggs, beaten
10 oz bocconcini (baby
   mozzarella balls), drained
vegetable oil, for deep-frying
salt and pepper

For the fresh pesto aioli

⅓ cup fresh store-bought
   green pesto
1 cup mayonnaise
2 garlic cloves, crushed

- Make the pesto aioli by mixing together all the ingredients. Set aside.

- In a medium bowl, mix together the bread crumbs, lemon zest, crushed red pepper, thyme, and some seasoning. Place the flour in a second bowl and the eggs in a third.

- Pat the mozzarella balls dry with paper towels. Roll the balls first in flour, then dip in the egg, then roll in the bread crumb mixture. Repeat in the egg and bread crumbs to create a double layer.

- Fill a saucepan or deep-fat fryer halfway with vegetable oil. Just before serving, heat over high heat until it reaches 350°F or a cube of bread sizzles and turns golden in 10–15 seconds. Using a strainer or slotted spoon, lower the crumbed mozzarella into the hot oil and fry for 3–4 minutes, until golden brown. Remove and drain on paper towels.

- Serve immediately with the fresh pesto aioli.

Tomato, Bocconcini, and Basil Tricolor Salad Slice 4 tomatoes and place in a wide salad bowl with a small handful basil and 10 oz bocconcini. Drizzle with ¼ cup extra virgin olive oil and squeeze the juice of 1 lemon over the top. Season well and serve with ciabatta bread.

Pasta, Boccacino, and Pesto Gratin Cook 12 oz penne according to the package directions. Meanwhile, heat 2 cups milk until bubbling. Place 3 tablespoons cornstarch in a small dish and pour over ⅓ cup of the hot milk. Mix together to form a paste and return to the milk pan. Stir the milk over low heat until it starts to thicken. Add 5 oz bocconcini, chopped, and season well with salt, black pepper, and grated nutmeg. Stir in ¼ cup fresh green pesto. In a separate saucepan, wilt 3 cups spinach and strain out all the liquid. Drain the pasta and add to the cheese sauce. Mix in the spinach and a pinch of crushed red pepper and transfer to an ovenproof gratin dish. Sprinkle ⅓ cup shredded mozzarella over the top and place under a hot broiler for 5 minutes or until golden and bubbling. Serve immediately.

Potato Blinis with Beet and Chives

Serves 4

1 cup mashed potatoes
⅓ cup self-rising flour
3 extra-large eggs, separated
2 tablespoons sour cream
¼ cup finely chopped dill
salt and pepper

For the topping

2 cooked beet, peeled and
   finely diced
⅓ cup crème fraîche
1 tablespoon creamed horseradish
salt and pepper
chopped chives, to garnish

- Place the mashed potatoes in a mixing bowl. Beat in the flour, egg yolks, sour cream, and dill and season well.

- Whisk the egg whites until stiff. Using a metal spoon, carefully fold the beaten egg whites into the potato mixture.

- Heat a little oil in a large, nonstick skillet. Add 3–4 separate tablespoons of the potato blini mixture. Cook over medium heat until set, then turn the potato blinis over and cook briefly so that both sides are lightly browned. Remove and keep warm. Repeat the process until all the potato mixture has been used.

- Meanwhile mix together the beet, crème fraîche, and creamed horseradish and season well.

- To serve, spoon the beet mixture over the blinis and garnish with chopped chives and freshly ground black pepper.

---

10 Beet and Chive Mashed Potatoes Blanch ¾ cup finely shredded curly kale in boiling water for 1 minute. Drain and reserve. Add 1 cup chopped chives and 2 coarsely grated, cooked beets to a food processor with the drained kale and process for 10–15 seconds. Meanwhile, reheat 2 cups cooked mashed potatoes, or prepare a similar quantity of instant mashed potatoes according to the package directions, and transfer to a mixing bowl. Add the kale mixture and 1 tablespoon whole-grain mustard. Season and mix well. Serve piping hot with steamed vegetables of your choice.

20 Potato and Chive Soup Melt 2 tablespoons butter in a saucepan. When it begins to foam, add 1 diced onion and toss in the butter until well coated. Stir in 2 cups cooked mashed potato or prepared instant mashed potatoes and 3¾ cups hot vegetable stock. Bring to a boil and add ½ cup milk. Puree the soup with an immersion blender. Season to taste. Stir in 3 tablespoons each finely chopped dill and chives. Season and serve immediately with crusty bread.

10 Spiced Paneer Bruschettas

Serves 4

7 oz fresh paneer (Indian cheese)
  or feta cheese, coarsely chopped
3 tablespoons finely chopped
  red onion
1 green chile, seeded and
  finely sliced
large handful fresh cilantro, finely
  chopped
4 baby plum tomatoes, quartered
2 tablespoons extra virgin olive oil,
  plus extra for drizzling (optional)
juice and finely grated zest
  of 1 lime
12 slices ciabatta bread
salt and pepper

- Place the cheese in a mixing bowl. Add the onions, chile, cilantro, tomatoes, olive oil, lime juice, and lime zest and season. Stir well and let sit while you toast or grill the ciabatta slices.

- Spoon the cheese mixture over the toasted ciabatta slices and serve immediately, drizzled with extra olive oil, if desired.

---

20 Spiced Paneer Kebabs Cut 1 lb paneer into 2 inch cubes. Sprinkle with 1 tablespoon each of chili powder and sea salt. Toss everything together and make sure the paneer is evenly coated. Combine 2 tablespoons chickpea (besan) flour with 2 teaspoons cumin seeds and ⅓ cup heavy cream. Coat the cubes in the spiced cream and marinate for 10 minutes. Thread onto 4 metal skewers and cook under a preheated hot broiler for 1–2 minutes on each side. Serve garnished with chopped cilantro and a salad.

30 Palak Paneer (Spinach with Indian Cheese) Cook 1⅓ cups basmati rice or long-grain rice according to the package directions. Blanch 8 oz baby spinach leaves in boiling water for 1–2 minutes or until wilted. Drain in a colander and run under cold water until cool. Process to a smooth paste in a food processor or blender, then set aside. Heat 3 tablespoons vegetable oil in a large nonstick pan. Add 2 teaspoons cumin seeds and cook for about 30 seconds, until fragrant, then add 1 chopped onion and cook over low heat for about 5–6 minutes, until soft. Add 1 tablespoon each of grated ginger and garlic and 1 chopped green chile and cook for another minute. Add 2 teaspoons ground coriander and salt to taste. Cook for another 30 seconds, then add the spinach and 8 oz cubed paneer, ½ teaspoon garam masala, and ¼ cup heavy cream. Stir and cook for another few minutes or until the spinach is creamy. Stir in the juice of 1 lemon to taste. Serve with the cooked rice.

Scallion Hash Browns with Avocado, Onion, and Tomato Salsa

Serves 4

7 boiled potatoes (such as russets or white rounders)

6 scallions, finely chopped

2 garlic cloves, very finely chopped

1 extra-large egg, lightly beaten

¼ cup sunflower oil

For the salsa

2 plum tomatoes, seeded and coarsely chopped

1 red chile, seeded and finely chopped

1 small red onion, halved and thinly sliced

¼ cup finely chopped fresh cilantro

2 avocados, peeled, pitted, and coarsely diced

juice of 2 limes

1 tablespoon avocado oil

lime wedges, to serve

- First make the salsa by mixing all the ingredients together in a bowl. Season well and set aside until ready to serve.

- Peel and coarsely grate the potatoes. Add the scallions, garlic, and egg and use your fingers to combine evenly.

- Heat a large, nonstick skillet over high heat and add half of the oil.

- Working in batches, divide the potato mixture into 8 portions. Spoon 4 of the portions in to the oil and pat down to form hash browns about 3¼–4 inches in diameter. Cook for 3–4 minutes on each side and then carefully transfer to a large nonstick baking sheet. Repeat with the remaining oil and potato mixture to make 8 hash browns.

- Serve the hash browns accompanied the salsa and the lime wedges.

Scallion and Potato Broth Place 12 sliced scallions, 2 cups cooked, cubed potatoes, 2 crushed garlic cloves, ¼ cup chopped cilantro, 2½ cups hot vegetable stock, and 2 cups milk in a saucepan. Bring to a boil and cook for 5–6 minutes or until piping hot. Season and serve immediately.

Fresh Salsa and Pasta Salad Cook 10 oz short pasta shapes according to the package directions. Meanwhile finely chop 4 plum tomatoes, 1 red chile, 1 red onion, and ⅓ cup cilantro and place in a wide bowl. Peel, pit, and coarsely dice 2 avocados and add to the bowl with the drained pasta. Drizzle ¼ cup extra virgin olive oil over teh top along wtih the juice of 2 limes. Season, toss to mix well, and serve.

Corn and Zucchini Cakes

Serves 4

1 cup fresh corn kernels

1 zucchini, coarsely grated

1 teaspoon cumin seeds

4 scallions, thinly sliced

3 tablespoons self-rising flour

2 eggs, beaten

2 tablespoons chopped
fresh cilantro

1 red chile, seeded and
coarsely chopped

vegetable oil, for shallow-frying

salt and pepper

To serve

store-bought guacamole

lime wedges

- Place the corn in a large bowl with the zucchini, cumin seeds, scallions, flour, eggs, cilantro, chile, and some seasoning and mix well.

- Heat a tablespoon of oil in a large nonstick skillet and cook spoonfuls of the mixture in batches for 2–3 minutes on each side, until cooked through. You should end up with 12 cakes, 3 for each person.

- Serve with guacamole and lime wedges.

---

1 Corn and Mixed Greens Salad

Add 1 (11½ oz) can corn kernels to a salad bowl with a coarsely grated zucchini and 1 (4 oz) package mixed salad greens. Pour over ⅓ cup store-bought Italian-style vinaigrette, season, toss to mix well, and serve.

---

3 Creamy Zucchini and Corn Pasta Casserole Cook 8 oz dried rigatoni according to the package directions, drain, and set aside in a large mixing bowl. Meanwhile, heat 2 tablespoons olive oil in a large skillet and sauté 1 chopped onion and 2 chopped garlic cloves for 1–2 minutes. Add 1 finely diced zucchini and 2¾ cups fresh corn kernels and stir-fry for another minute or so. Mix 1 cup crème fraîche with 2 beaten eggs and 1 tablespoon Dijon mustard. Season well and add to the pasta with the vegetable mixture and ¼ cup chopped fresh cilantro. Mix well, transfer to a shallow ovenproof dish, and bake in a preheated oven, at 400°F, for 12–15 minutes. Remove from the oven and serve immediately.

Vegetable Spring Rolls

Serves 4

1 tablespoon peanut oil

2 garlic cloves, finely chopped

small piece of fresh ginger, grated

1 red chile, seeded and finely chopped

1 (10 oz) package mixed stir-fry vegetables

1 tablespoon soy sauce

1 tablespoon rice wine vinegar

4 sheets phyllo pastry, each cut into 4 rectangles (about 6 x 5 inches)

4 tablespoons salted butter, melted

sweet chili sauce, to serve

- Heat a wok over high heat and add the oil, garlic, ginger, and chile, then stir-fry for 30 seconds. Add the mixed vegetables, soy sauce, and vinegar and cook for 1 minute. Spoon the vegetables into a strainer over a bowl and let cool slightly.

- Place a spoonful of the vegetable mixture in the center of the narrow edge of a phyllo rectangle. Roll the phyllo around the mixture until halfway along the phyllo sheet, then fold each side of unfilled pastry into the center. Continue rolling into a cylinder and brush with butter to seal. Repeat with the remaining pastry sheets.

- Place the spring rolls on a baking sheet and brush with butter. Bake in a preheated oven, at 400°F, for 12–15 minutes, until golden and crisp. Serve hot with sweet chili sauce.

---

10 Vegetable Fried Rice

Heat 2 tablespoons vegetable oil in a large skillet or wok over high heat. Add 2 chopped garlic cloves, 1 teaspoon coarsely grated ginger, 2½ cups cooked white rice, and 1 (10 oz) package mixed stir-fry vegetables. Stir-fry over high heat for 5–6 minutes or until piping hot. Stir in ⅓ cup light soy sauce, 1 tablespoon sesame oil, and 1 teaspoon chili oil. Remove from the heat, stir in the juice of 1 lime, and serve immediately.

20 Thai Noodle and Vegetable Stir-Fry

Cover 8 oz thin rice noodles with boiling water in a bowl, cover, and let stand for 5 minutes (or prepare the noodles according to the package directions), then drain. Meanwhile, add 1 tablespoon vegetable oil to a large wok and place over high heat. Add 2 teaspoons coarsely grated fresh ginger, 2 chopped garlic cloves, 8 thinly sliced scallions, and 1 red chile and stir-fry for 1 minute. Add 1 (10 oz) package mixed stir-fry vegetables and cook for 3–4 minutes. Mix together ¼ cup each of sweet chili sauce and hoisin sauce with ¼ cup water and add to the wok. Stir-fry for another 3–4 minutes. Add the drained noodles along with 3 tablespoons each of chopped mint and cilantro and toss to mix well. Serve immediately in shallow bowls.

Deviled Eggs with Capers

Serves 4

6 eggs
1 teaspoon smoked paprika,
  plus extra to sprinkle
3 tablespoons mayonnaise
1 teaspoon English mustard
salt and pepper

To garnish

1 tablespoon small capers
1 tablespoon pink peppercorns,
  in brine, drained
thyme sprigs

- Place the eggs in a saucepan of salted water and bring to a boil. Cook for about 10–15 minutes, until they are hard boiled. Remove from the water and let cool.

- Shell the eggs and cut in half lengthwise.

- Scoop out the egg yolks and mash them together in a small mixing bowl. Mix in the paprika, mayonnaise, and mustard and season well.

- Spoon the egg yolk mixture back into the egg white halves and garnish with the small capers, pink peppercorns, and thyme sprigs. Sprinkle with paprika and serve.

---

1 **Spicy Fried Eggs with Chapattis** Heat 2 tablespoons sunflower oil in a large skillet over medium heat. Carefully break 4 extra-large eggs into the skillet and fry for 2–3 minutes, or until cooked to your liking. Meanwhile, warm 4 chapattis in the microwave or warm oven. Place onto 4 warm plates and top each chapatti with a fried egg. To serve, season and sprinkle with a mixture of 2 teaspoons dried crushed red pepper, 1 teaspoon smoked paprika, 1 tablespoon small capers, and 2 tablespoons finely chopped flat leaf parsley.

2 **Spicy Scrambled Eggs** Melt 2 tablespoons butter in a skillet and cook 1 finely chopped onion and 3 chopped garlic cloves for 4–5 minutes, until soft. Add 2 teaspoons cumin seeds, 1 teaspoon each of curry powder and ground turmeric, and 1 chopped red chile and cook for another 4–5 minutes, until fragrant and well combined. Add 2 finely chopped tomatoes and cook for another 3–4 minutes, until softened. Beat 8 eggs with ½ cup light cream in a bowl, then add the mixture to the skillet and cook, stirring continuously, until the eggs are just set. While the eggs are cooking, toast 4 large slices of sourdough bread and keep warm. Stir 2 tablespoons finely chopped cilantro into the eggs, spoon the eggs onto the toast, and serve immediately.

QuickCook

Substantial Soups and Salads

Recipes listed by cooking time

3O

2O

3⦾ Spiced Potato, Cilantro, and Celeriac Soup

Serves 4

1 onion, chopped

2 tablespoons olive oil

1 garlic clove, chopped

½ teaspoon each of ground
   cumin and coriander

pinch of crushed red pepper

2 small celeriac, peeled and
   finely diced

2 medium potatoes, peeled
   and finely diced

4 cups hot vegetable stock

½ cup chopped cilantro

¼ cup crème fraîche or
   plain Greek yogurt, to serve

toasted cumin seeds, to garnish

· Place the onion and olive oil in a saucepan with the garlic, ground cumin, ground coriander, and crushed red pepper. Cook over medium heat for 1 minute.

· Add the celeriac and potato, cover with the hot vegetable stock, and bring to a boil. Simmer for 15–20 minutes or until the vegetables are tender.

· Stir in the chopped cilantro and blend with an immersion blender until fairly smooth.

· Serve in warm bowls with a dollop of crème fraîche and toasted cumin seeds.

1⦾ Asian-Style Celeriac, Carrot, and Cabbage Slaw In a large bowl, mix 1 coarsely shredded celeriac with 2 coarsely shredded carrots, ½ finely shredded red cabbage, and a large handful of chopped cilantro. Mix together ½ cup crème fraîche or plain Greek yogurt with ⅔ cup mayonnaise, 1 teaspoon each of ground cumin, ground coriander, and dried crushed red pepper, and the juice of 2 limes. Season, pour over the celeriac mixture, toss to mix well, and serve.

2⦾ Spicy Potato and Celeriac Stir-Fry Heat ¼ cup vegetable oil in a large skillet or wok and add 1 chopped onion, 1 chopped garlic clove, 1 teaspoon each of cumin and crushed coriander seeds, and 1 chopped red chile. Stir-fry over medium heat for 2–3 minutes. Add 1 large coarsely shredded potato and 1 large coarsely shredded celeriac. Stir-fry over high heat for 10–12 minutes or until the potato and celeriac are cooked through and tender. Remove from the heat and stir in a large handful of chopped cilantro. Season and serve.

Beet and Apple Soup

Serves 4

1 tablespoon olive oil

1 tablespoon butter

2 Granny Smith apples, peeled, cored, and chopped

1 apple, such as Pippin, peeled, cored, and chopped

4½ cups coarsely chopped cooked beet

2 teaspoons caraway seeds

4–5 fresh thyme sprigs

6½ cups vegetable stock

salt and pepper

crème fraîche or plain Greek yogurt, to serve

chopped dill, to garnish

- Heat the oil and butter in a saucepan and cook the apples for 2–3 minutes, until golden. Add the cooked beet, caraway seeds, and thyme and stir-fry for 1–2 minutes.

- Add the stock, bring to a boil, then cook for 10 minutes.

- In a blender or with an immersion blender, process the soup until fairly smooth and season to taste.

- Serve in bowls with crème fraîche swirled through. Garnish with chopped dill and freshly ground black pepper.

---

10 Beet and Apple Salad

Thinly slice 6 large, cooked beets and place on a wide salad platter with 4 cored and sliced apples, such as Red Delicious or Pink Lady, and the leaves of 2 heads of raddichio. Whisk together ⅓ cup olive oil, 2 tablespoons cider vinegar, 1 teaspoon honey, 1 teaspoon thyme leaves, ½ teaspoon caraway seeds, and 1 teaspoon Dijon mustard. Season and drizzle this dressing over the salad. Toss to mix well and serve.

---

30 Beet and Apple Roast Cut 6 large, cooked beet into wedges and place in a roasting pan with 6 peeled, cored apples, such as Jonagold or Pippin, cut into wedges. Drizzle with ¼ cup olive oil and add 4 thyme sprigs. Sprinkle 2 teaspoons caraway seeds over the top and roast for 15–20 minutes. Serve immediately over a bed of rice or couscous.

 Chunky Mushroom Soup

Serves 4

2 tablespoons butter
1 large onion, chopped
1 leek, finely sliced
2 garlic cloves, crushed
5 cups coarsely chopped
  cremini mushrooms
2 tablespoons all-purpose flour
2 cups vegetable stock
1¾ cups milk
1 tablespoon finely chopped
  tarragon
salt and pepper
crusty bread, to serve

- Melt the butter in a saucepan over low heat and gently cook the onion, leek, and garlic until they start to soften.

- Increase the heat and add the mushrooms to the pan, stirring until well combined. Continue to stir-fry for 2–3 minutes.

- Stir in the flour and continue to cook for 1 minute.

- Remove the pan from the heat and add the stock a little at a time, stirring well between each addition.

- Once all the stock is added, return the pan to the heat, bring to a boil, reduce the heat, and simmer for a few minutes.

- Pour in the milk and bring to a simmer. Stir in the chopped tarragon and season to taste.

- Ladle the soup into bowls and serve with crusty bread.

---

1 **Mushroom Stir-Fry**
Heat 2 tablespoons butter in a large wok and add 5 cups sliced cremini mushrooms, 2 chopped garlic cloves, 1 sliced onion, and 1 sliced leek. Stir-fry over high heat for 6–8 minutes, remove from the heat, stir in ¼ cup light soy sauce, and serve over noodles or rice.

 2 **Mushroom, Leek, and Tarragon Open Omelet** Heat 2 tablespoons butter in a large, nonstick skillet and add 1 finely chopped leek, 2 chopped garlic cloves, and 5 cups finely chopped cremini mushrooms. Stir-fry for 2–3 minutes, then pour in 6 beaten eggs. Season, sprinkle with 1 tablespoon chopped tarragon, and cook for 6–8 minutes or until the bottom is just set. Place the skillet under a preheated hot broiler for 3–4 minutes or until golden and puffed. Serve immediately with crusty bread and a salad.

Lettuce, Pea, and Tarragon Soup

Serves 4

2 tablespoons butter
8 scallions, trimmed and sliced
5½ cups frozen peas
1 tablespoon chopped
   tarragon leaves
1 romaine lettuce, finely shredded
4 cups hot vegetable stock
2 tablespoons heavy cream
salt and pepper
tarragon sprigs, to garnish
   (optional)

- Melt the butter in a large saucepan over medium heat. Add the scallions and cook, stirring continuously, for 2 minutes.

- Stir in the peas, ½ of the tarragon, and the lettuce. Cook for 1 minute.

- Add the stock, bring to a boil, cover, and simmer for 5 minutes or until tender.

- Pour the soup into a blender, add the remaining tarragon, and process until smooth. Season to taste.

- Divide the soup among 4 bowls, swirl the cream into each bowl, and sprinkle with black pepper. Garnish with tarragon sprigs, if liked.

Lettuce, Pea, Tomato, and Scallion Salad Separate the leaves of 2 washed romaine lettuce and place in a large, wide salad bowl with 8 sliced scallions, 4 sliced plum tomatoes, 3¾ cups blanched peas, and 12 sliced radishes. Make a dressing by whisking together the juice of 1 lemon, ⅓ cup olive oil, 1 teaspoon Dijon mustard, 2 tablespoons finely chopped tarragon, and 2 teaspoons honey. Season and pour over the salad ingredients. Toss to mix well and serve.

Quinoa and Lettuce Tabouleh Put 1 cup quinoa in a saucepan and dry-fry for 2–3 minutes. Add 2½ cups hot vegetable stock, bring to a boil, and stir to mix well. Reduce the heat and cook for 15–20 minutes or until all the liquid has been absorbed. Meanwhile, coarsely chopped the leaves of 1 romaine lettuce and add to a wide salad bowl with 6 finely chopped scallions, ¼ cup each of finely chopped tarragon and parsley, and 3 cups blanched peas. Transfer the quinoa to the bowl and drizzle ⅓ cup olive oil over the top with the juice of 1 orange. Season, toss to mix well, and serve.

Hearty Minestrone

Serves 4

3 carrots, coarsely chopped
1 red onion, coarsely chopped
6 celery sticks, coarsely chopped
2 tablespoons olive oil
2 garlic cloves, crushed
2 potatoes, peeled and cut into
   ½ inch dice
¼ cup tomato paste
6½ cups vegetable stock
1 (14½ oz) can diced tomatoes
5 oz short pasta shapes
1 (15 oz) can cannellini beans,
   drained
3½ cups baby spinach
salt and pepper

- Process the carrots, onion, and celery in a food processor until finely chopped.

- Heat the oil in a large saucepan, add the chopped vegetables, garlic, potatoes, tomato paste, stock, diced tomatoes, and pasta. Bring to a boil, reduce the heat, and simmer, covered, for 12–15 minutes.

- Add the cannellini beans and spinach for the final 2 minutes of the cooking time.

- Season to taste and serve with crusty bread.

---

1  Bean, Spinach, and Pasta Salad

Drain 1 (15 oz) can cannellini beans and add the beans to a large, wide bowl with 3½ cups baby spinach, 2 coarsely shredded carrots, ½ thinly sliced red onion, and 4 cups cooked short pasta shapes. Pour over ⅓ cup store-bought Italian-style vinaigrette, toss to mix well, and serve.

2 Chunky Pasta Sauce

Heat 2 tablespoons olive oil in a large skillet and add 2 chopped garlic cloves, 1 chopped red onion, 2 chopped celery sticks, 1 chopped carrot, and 1 (14½ oz) can diced tomatoes. Bring to a boil and simmer for 12–15 minutes. Meanwhile, cook 12 oz short pasta shapes according to the package directions. Stir 3½ cups baby spinach into the sauce with 1¼ cups drained cannellini beans. Season well and serve over the cooked pasta with grated Parmesan.

Iced Green Gazpacho

Serves 4

2 celery sticks (including leaves)
1 small green bell pepper, seeded
1 large cucumber, peeled
3 slices stale white bread,
   crusts removed
1 fresh green chile, seeded
4 garlic cloves
1 teaspoon honey
1¼ cups walnuts, lightly toasted
7 cups baby spinach
2 cups basil
¼ cup cider vinegar
1 cup extra virgin olive oil, plus
   extra for drizzling
⅓ cup plain yogurt
2 cups iced water
handful of ice cubes
salt and pepper
store-bought croutons, to serve

- Coarsely chopped the celery, bell pepper, cucumber, bread, chile, and garlic.

- Place in a blender and add the honey, walnuts, spinach, basil, vinegar, oil, yogurt, most of the iced water, and the ice cubes and season well. Process the soup until smooth. Add more iced water, if needed, to achieve the desired consistency.

- Taste the soup and adjust the seasoning, if necessary.

- Serve in chilled bowls and garnish with croutons and a drizzle of olive oil.

Green Vegetable Salad Place 4 finely sliced celery sticks, 1 sliced cucumber, 1 thinly sliced green bell pepper, and 3½ cups baby spinach into a large, wide bowl. Make a dressing by whisking ⅔ cup plain yogurt in a bowl with the juice of 1 lime, 1 crushed garlic clove, 1 teaspoon honey, and 1 finely diced green chile. Drizzle the salad with the dressing and scatter with a small handful of store-bought croutons before serving.

Spiced Green Pilaf with Walnuts Heat 3 tablespoons olive oil in a saucepan and add 4 crushed garlic cloves, 1 finely chopped green bell pepper, 2 chopped green chiles, and 8 sliced scallions. Stir-fry for 5–6 minutes. Stir in 7 cups coarsely chopped baby spinach and 2 teaspoons cumin seeds. Stir-fry for another 3–4 minutes or until the spinach has wilted. Add 4 cups cold, cooked basmati rice or long-grain rice, season well, and stir-fry for 3–4 minutes or until piping hot. Serve immediately garnished with ¾ cup chopped, toasted walnuts.

 # Jamaican Spiced Corn Chowder

Serves 4

1 tablespoon olive oil

1 large onion, finely chopped

2 garlic cloves, finely chopped

1 teaspoon cayenne pepper

1 cup red split lentils, rinsed

4 cups hot vegetable stock

1¾ cups coconut milk

1 Scotch bonnet chile, left whole

1 tablespoon thyme leaves

2 potatoes, peeled and cut into
  ½ inch dice

3 carrots, peeled and cut into
  ½ inch dice

2½ cups corn kernels (either
  fresh, frozen, or canned)

2 red bell peppers, cut into
  ½ inch dice

salt and pepper

chopped cilantro, to garnish

- Heat the oil in a saucepan and stir-fry the onion and garlic for 2–3 minutes.

- Increase the heat and add the cayenne pepper, red lentils, stock, coconut milk, chile, thyme, potato, and carrots. Bring to a boil and simmer for 15–20 minutes.

- Season and add the corn and red bell pepper for the last 3 minutes of the cooking time.

- Remove the Scotch bonnet chile, ladle the chowder into warm bowls, and serve garnished with chopped cilantro and sprinkled with freshly ground black pepper.

---

1 Corn and Red Bell Pepper Curry

Heat 1 tablespoon olive oil in a saucepan and sauté 1 chopped onion and 2 chopped garlic cloves with 4 cups corn kernels and 2 finely diced red bell peppers for 1–2 minutes. Add 1 tablespoon mild curry powder and 2½ cups coconut milk and bring to a boil. Cook for 3–4 minutes, remove from the heat, and stir in ¼ cup finely chopped fresh cilantro before serving over rice.

2 Spicy Corn Hash

Heat 1 tablespoon olive oil in a large skillet. Add 1 chopped onion, 2 chopped garlic cloves, ¼ chopped Scotch bonnet chile (you might want to wear dish-washing gloves because they're extremely hot), and 1 teaspoon cayenne pepper. Stir-fry for 1–2 minutes, then add 1 cup coarsely shredded potato, 2 cups coarsely shredded carrots, 4 cups corn kernels, and 1 finely diced red pepper.

Add 1 cup coconut milk, stir, and cook over high heat for 10 minutes or until the liquid has evaporated and the vegetables are tender. Garnish with chopped fresh cilantro before serving with crusty bread and a fried egg, if desired.

Asian Rice Soup with Egg and Greens

Serves 4

4 scallions
1½ cups coarsely chopped
  bok choy
2 tablespoons vegetable oil
1 inch piece fresh ginger root,
  finely grated
2 garlic cloves, finely chopped
1 cup jasmine rice
½ cup rice wine
2 tablespoons soy sauce
1 teaspoon rice wine vinegar
4 cups hot vegetable stock
4 eggs
1 tablespoon chili oil, for drizzling

- Finely slice the scallions, keeping the white and green parts separate. Combine the green parts with the bok choy in a bowl and set aside.

- Heat the oil gently in a saucepan. When hot, add the scallion whites, ginger, and garlic and stir-fry for 2–3 minutes.

- Add the rice, stir, then add the wine and simmer for a minute or so.

- Add the soy sauce, vinegar, and stock and simmer, stirring occasionally, for 10–12 minutes. Then stir in the reserved scallions and bok choy and cook for another 2–3 minutes. Meanwhile poach the eggs in two batches.

- To serve, ladle the soup into 4 shallow soup bowls and top each one with a poached egg and drizzle with the chili oil.

Asian Rice and Greens Salad

Place 4 cups blanched and coarsely chopped bok choy in a salad bowl with 6 sliced scallions and 2½ cups cooked jasmine rice. Make a dressing by whisking together 1 crushed garlic clove, 1 teaspoon grated ginger, ¼ teaspoon chili oil, 2 tablespoons light soy sauce, the juice of 2 limes, a dash of rice wine vinegar, and ¼ cup vegetable oil. Season, pour over the salad, and toss to mix well before serving.

Egg Noodle and Vegetable Stir-Fry

Heat 2 tablespoons vegetable oil in a large wok and add 8 sliced scallions, 1 sliced red bell pepper, 2 chopped garlic cloves, 1 teaspoon finely chopped fresh ginger root. Stir-fry over medium heat for 3–4 minutes. Add 6 cups coarsely chopped bok choy and stir-fry for 2–3 minutes. In a bowl mix together 1 tablespoon cornstarch with ⅓ cup light soy sauce, ½ cup vegetable stock, 1 teaspoon chili oil, and ¼ cup rice wine vinegar. Pour into the wok, turn the heat to high, and cook for 2–3 minutes. Meanwhile, cook 12 oz fresh egg noodles according to the package directions. Add the noodles to the vegetables, toss to mix well, and heat until piping hot. Serve immediately.

VEG-SOUP-PES

Spinach and Red Lentil Soup

Serves 4

1⅓ cups dried red lentils

3 tablespoons sunflower oil

1 large onion, finely chopped

2 garlic cloves, crushed

1 inch piece fresh ginger root, grated

1 red chile, seeded and chopped, plus extra to garnish (optional)

1 tablespoon medium curry powder

1¼ cups hot vegetable stock

¾ cup canned tomatoes

3½ cups baby leaf spinach

½ cup chopped cilantro, plus extra to garnish

½ cup half-and-half mixed with ¼ teaspoon vanilla extract

salt and pepper

¼ cup plain yogurt, to serve

- Put the lentils into medium saucepan and cover with 4 cups cold water. Bring to a boil, skim off the scum as it rises to the surface, and let simmer for 10 minutes, until the lentils are tender and just falling apart. Remove from the heat, cover, and set aside.

- Meanwhile, heat the oil in a large saucepan, add the onion, and cook gently for 5 minutes. Add the garlic, ginger, and chile and cook for 2 minutes. Stir in the curry powder and ½ teaspoon black pepper and cook for another 2 minutes.

- Add the stock, the lentils and their cooking liquid, the tomatoes, spinach, and cilantro and season with salt. Cover and simmer for 5 minutes, then add the vanilla-flavored half-and-half.

- Process the mixture with an immersion blender until the soup is almost smooth.

- Ladle the soup into 4 warm bowls and garnish each with a spoonful of yogurt, the remaining cilantro, freshly ground black pepper, and finely chopped red chile, if desired.

---

1 **Spinach, Green Lentil, and Yellow Rice Pilaf** Heat 1 tablespoon oil in a large wok and add 1 chopped onion, 2 chopped garlic cloves, 1 teaspoon grated ginger, 1 chopped red chile, and 1 tablespoon curry powder. Stir-fry for 1–2 minutes, then add 2½ cups cooked instant long-grain rice, 3 cups chopped baby spinach, and ½ cup hot vegetable stock. Stir and cook over high heat for 5–6 minutes or until piping hot. Add in 1 cup drained, canned green lentils and stir. Cook until warm through. Season and serve warm, with plain yogurt.

2 **Spinach, Tomato, and Coconut Curry** Heat 2 tablespoons oil in a saucepan. Add 1 chopped onion, 2 chopped garlic cloves, 1 teaspoon grated ginger, 1 red chile, chopped, and 1 tablespoon curry powder and stir-fry for 1–2 minutes. Add 2⅓ cups chopped tomatoes, 1 cup coconut milk, and 1 (10 oz) package spinach. Stir, season, and cook over medium heat for 10–12 minutes, until the spinach wilts. Stir in ½ cup of chopped cilantro and serve with long-grain rice.

Mixed Beans and Baby Spinach Salad with Avocado Dressing

Serves 4

5 cups baby spinach

1 large carrot, coarsely shredded

2 medium tomatoes, quartered

1 small red bell pepper, seeded and thinly sliced

1½ cups mixed canned beans, such as black-eyed peas, pinto beans, red kidney beans, and azuki beans, drained

½ cup canned chickpeas, drained

2 tablespoons pumpkin seeds, lightly toasted

For the avocado dressing

1 ripe avocado

1 teaspoon Dijon mustard

juice of 1 lemon

1 teaspoon honey

dash of Tabasco sauce

¼ cup extra virgin olive oil

salt and pepper

- Mix the baby spinach and carrot together and place onto a wide salad platter or into a large bowl.

- Add the tomatoes and bell pepper slices, then scatter the mixed beans, chickpeas, and toasted pumpkin seeds over the top.

- Halve the avocado and remove the pit. Scoop the flesh into a food processor and add the mustard, lemon juice, honey, and Tabasco sauce. Blend until smooth, then, with the motor still running, gradually pour in the oil and 2–3 tablespoons warm water. Season to taste.

- Drizzle the dressing over the salad and serve immediately.

---

10 Rustic Mixed Bean and Spinach Soup

Heat 3¼ cups of canned cream of tomato soup in a large saucepan, add 1½ cups of drained, mixed canned beans (see above) and 7 cups chopped baby spinach, and bring to a boil. Simmer gently for 5–6 minutes, season, and serve immediately.

30 Individual Chickpea and Spinach Gratins

Heat 2 tablespoons olive oil in a large skillet and gently cook 1 chopped onion, ½ chopped red bell pepper, and 1 crushed garlic clove until soft. Add 2 teaspoons cumin seeds, 2 teaspoons crushed coriander seeds, and 1 teaspoon smoked paprika and cook for 1 minute. Add 2¼ cups chopped tomatoes and 5 cups chopped spinach along with ¾ cups drained, canned chickpeas and ¾ cup drained, mixed canned beans (see above). Bring to a boil and simmer for 5 minutes. Whisk 1 cup plain yogurt and stir into the vegetable mixture. Season well and transfer to 4 deep individual pie or baking dishes. Sprinkle over 1 cup shredded cheddar cheese and bake in a preheated oven, at 425°F, for 10–15 minutes or until piping hot.

Tricolor Avocado and Couscous Salad

Serves 4

1 cup couscous

1¼ cups hot vegetable stock
or boiling water

1¾ cups cherry tomatoes

2 avocados, peeled, pitted,
and chopped

5 oz mozzarella cheese, drained
and chopped

handful arugula

For the dressing

2 tablespoons fresh green pesto

1 tablespoon lemon juice

¼ cup extra virgin olive oil

salt and pepper

- Mix the couscous and stock (or boiling water) together in a bowl, then cover with a plate and let stand for 10 minutes.

- To make the dressing, mix the pesto with the lemon juice and season, then gradually mix in the oil. Pour over the couscous and mix with a fork.

- Add the tomatoes, avocados, and mozzarella to the couscous, mix well, then lightly stir in the arugula.

Italian-Style Ciabatta with Cherry Tomatoes, Avocado, and Mozzarella Mix together 2 chopped tomatoes, 2 chopped avocados, and 8 oz chopped mozzarella and season well. Halve and lighty toast 4 ciabatta rolls and spread with ½ cup store-bought pesto. Divide the avocado mixture among the rolls, garnish with a few arugula leaves, and serve.

Cherry Tomato, Avocado, and Mozzarella Pasta Place 2 cups finely chopped cherry tomatoes, 2 finely chopped avocados, 2 cups finely chopped arugula, and 8 oz finely chopped mozzarella cheese in a bowl with ⅓ cup store-bought pesto and 2 tablespoons olive oil. Season and stir to mix well. Let stand at room temperature for 15 minutes for the flavors to blend. Meanwhile, cook 12 oz spaghetti according to the package directions. Drain the pasta and transfer to a wide serving dish. Add the cherry tomato mixture, toss to mix well, and serve.

Serves 4

2 red apples, cored and diced
4 celery sticks, thinly sliced
1 head of romaine lettuce, leaves
    washed and coarsely torn
4 scallions, thinly sliced
bunch of chives, chopped
4 hard-boiled eggs, shelled and
    halved, to garnish

For the croutons

2 slices of crusty bread, cubed
2 teaspoons garlic salt
2 teaspoons dried mixed herbs
3 tablespoons olive oil

For the dressing

2 garlic cloves, crushed
2 tablespoons capers, drained
2 tablespoons lemon juice
2 teaspoons Dijon mustard
1 teaspoon sugar or honey
½ cup grated Parmesan cheese
½ cup plain yogurt
salt and pepper

- First make the croutons. Place the cubes of bread into a bowl and sprinkle with the garlic salt and dried herbs. Drizzle with the olive oil and toss to coat evenly.

- Place the croutons on a baking sheet in a single layer and bake in a preheated oven, at 400°F, for 10–12 minutes or until lightly browned and crisp. Remove from the oven and set aside.

- Meanwhile make the dressing. Place the garlic, capers, lemon juice, mustard, sugar or honey, Parmesan, and yogurt in a blender and process unti smooth. Season with black pepper. Chill until ready to use (you can make the dressing up to a day in advance, if desired).

- Place the apples, celery, lettuce, scallions, and chives in a wide salad bowl.

- Drizzle the dressing over the salad ingredients and toss to mix well.

- Garnish with the halved eggs and top with the garlic and herb croutons.

---

1 Crisp Lettuce Salad with Croutons

Place the leaves from 2 romaine lettuce in a bowl with 6 sliced scallions, 2 sliced celery sticks, and 1 sliced cucumber. Drizzle with ½ cup store-bought Caesar salad dressing, scatter with 3 cups store-bought croutons, season, toss to mix well, and serve.

2 Caesar-Style Pasta Salad

Cook 8 oz pennette or other short pasta shapes according to the package directions. Meanwhile, coarsely chopped the leaves of 1 romaine lettuce, 6 scallions, 2 celery sticks, a small handful of chopped chives, and 4 hard-boiled eggs, putting them all in a wide salad bowl.

Drain the pasta and rinse under cold running water to cool, then drain and add to the salad mixture. Drizzle with ½ cup store-bought Caesar salad dressing (or use from the recipe above), season, toss to mix well, and serve.

Warm Pasta Salad with Lemon and Broccoli

Serves 4

12 oz penne or rigatoni

2 cups broccoli florets

⅔ cup frozen edamame (soybeans)

⅔ cup frozen peas

1½ cups sugarsnap peas, trimmed

⅔ cup cream cheese with garlic and herbs

finely grated zest and juice of 1 lemon

¼ cup olive oil

1 red chile, seeded and finely chopped

1 cup grated pecorino cheese

2 tablespoons chopped tarragon

salt and pepper

- Cook the pasta in a large saucepan following the package directions, and add the broccoli florets, edamame, peas, and sugarsnaps for the final 3 minutes of its cooking time.

- Drain the pasta and vegetables, saving a ladleful of the cooking water, then transfer back into the pan.

- Stir in the cream cheese, lemon zest and juice, olive oil, chile, pecorino, tarragon, some seasoning, and a splash of cooking water.

- Serve the salad warm or at room temperature.

Quick Broccoli and Vegetable Stir-Fry

Heat 2 tablespoons olive oil in a large wok. Add 4 cups blanched broccoli florets, ⅔ cup shelled edamame (soybeans), ⅔ cup peas, 1½ cups sugarsnap peas, 2 crushed garlic cloves, 1 chopped red chile, and 1 teaspoon grated fresh ginger root. Stir-fry over high heat for 4–5 minutes, then stir in ½ cup of a store-bought stir-fry sauce of your choice. Stir-fry for 2–3 minutes and serve immediately over cooked noodles.

Broccoli, Pasta, and Mixed Pea Casserole Put 1 lb rigatoni, cooked, into a greased ovenproof dish with 2 cups blanched broccoli florets, ⅔ cup peas, ⅔ cup shelled edamame (soybeans), and 1½ cups blanched sugarsnap peas. Toss to mix well. In a separate bowl, whisk together 3 eggs with 1 tablespoon finely grated lemon zest, 2 tablespoons finely chopped tarragon, 1 chopped red chile, and ⅔ cup cream cheese with garlic and herbs. Season well. Pour the egg mixture into the ovenproof dish, sprinkle with 1 cup grated pecorino cheese, and bake in a preheated oven, at 425°F, for 15–20 minutes or until the mixture is bubbling and lightly golden on the top. Serve hot or at room temperature.

30 Warm Moroccan Bulgur and Roasted Vegetable Salad

Serves 4

2 tablespoons harissa paste

2 tablespoons olive oil

4 cups diced butternut squash
and sweet potato

2 red bell peppers, seeded and
cut into bite-size pieces

1 cup bulgur wheat

2½ cups hot vegetable stock

2 garlic cloves, crushed

juice of 1 lemon

1 cup plain yogurt

⅓ cup each finely chopped
cilantro and mint

salt and pepper

· Mix the harissa paste and oil together in a bowl and add the squash, sweet potato, and red pepper and toss until well coated.

· Spread the vegetables on a large baking sheet and roast in a preheated oven, at 400°F, for 20 minutes, until softened and the edges of the vegetables are starting to char.

· Meanwhile, put the bulgur wheat in a large bowl and pour over the hot stock, then cover and let absorb the liquid for 15 minutes, until the grains are tender but still have a little bite.

· In a separate bowl, mix the garlic and lemon juice into the yogurt and season to taste.

· Let the bulgur wheat cool slightly, then toss in the roasted vegetables and chopped cilantro and mint. Serve warm with the yogurt mixture.

---

10 Superfast Harissa and Roasted Vegetable Soup Place the roasted vegetables from the recipe above in a blender with 2 cups hot vegetable stock, 1 tablespoon harissa paste, and 3 tablespoons each of chopped cilantro and mint. Blend until smooth and serve in warm bowls with a dollop of plain yogurt.

20 Middle Eastern Butternut and Sweet Potato Stew Heat 2 tablespoons oil in a saucepan and add 1 chopped onion, 2 chopped garlic cloves, 2 finely chopped red bell peppers, and 3 cups finely diced butternut squash and sweet potato. Stir-fry for 1–2 minutes. Add 2 cups hot vegetable stock and 1 tablespoon harissa paste and bring to a boil. Cook for 10–15 minutes or until the vegetables are tender. Season and stir in 2 tablespoons each of finely chopped cilantro and mint. Serve with cooked bulgur wheat or couscous.

Quail Egg Salad with Baby Spinach

20

Serves 4

3½ cups baby spinach
1 red onion, sliced
1⅓ cups halved yellow and
   red cherry tomatoes
1 tablespoon whole-grain
   mustard
⅓ cup avocado oil
juice of 1 lemon
1 teaspoon honey
12 quail eggs, hard boiled
   and shelled
salt and pepper

- Place the spinach, red onion, and tomatoes in a wide mixing bowl.

- In another bowl, mix together the mustard, oil, lemon juice, and honey. Season well and stir until well combined.

- Divide the salad among 4 serving plates.

- Halve 4 of the eggs, leaving the rest whole, and scatter over the top of the salad, the drizzle the dressing over each serving.

10   Ciabatta with Quail Eggs and Salad

Split 4 warm, individual ciabattas and spread each bottom with 2 tablespoons mayonnaise and 1 tablespoon whole-grain mustard. Mix together 1 sliced red onion, a small handful of baby spinach, and ⅔ cup sliced cherry tomatoes. Spoon this mixture over the ciabatta bottoms. Top with 12 halved hard-boiled quail eggs. Replace the lids and serve.

30   Warm Quail Egg and Rice Salad

Cook 1 cup instant rice according to the package directions. Meanwhile, place 3½ cups baby spinach in a wide salad bowl with 1 finely chopped red onion, 2¾ cups halved red and yellow cherry tomatoes, and 12 hard-boiled, shelled quail eggs. Make a dressing by whisking together ⅓ cup avocado oil with the juice of 1 lemon, 1 teaspoon honey, and 1 tablespoon whole-grain mustard and season well. Pour over the salad ingredients with the warm, cooked rice and a small handful of chopped flat leaf parsley. Toss to mix well and serve.

Watermelon, Olive, Green Bean, and Feta Salad

Serves 4

2¾ cups halved green beans
1 red onion
juice of 2 limes
3 lb ripe watermelon
8 oz feta cheese
1 cup pitted ripe black olives
1 bunch flat leaf parsley,
 coarsely chopped
1 bunch mint, coarsely chopped
⅓ cup extra virgin olive oil
salt and pepper

- Blanch the green beans in a saucepan of boiling water for 3 minutes. Drain, refresh under cold water, and set aside.

- Halve the red onion and cut into thin slices. Place in a small bowl with the drained beans and the lime juice and let steep. Season with salt.

- Remove the rind and seeds from the watermelon and cut into bite-size pieces. Cut the feta into pieces of a similar size and put them both into a large, wide, shallow bowl or serving dish.

- Add the red onions and beans, along with their juices, to the wide bowl or serving dish. Scatter with the olives and herbs.

- Season well with salt and pepper, drizzle with the olive oil, and serve at room temperature.

Moroccan Orange and Black Olive Salad with Feta Peel and segment 4 large oranges (saving any juices) and place them on a serving platter with 1 cup pitted ripe black olives and 8 oz cubed feta cheese. Drizzle with ¼ cup olive oil and sprinkle 2 teaspoons of Moroccan spice mix over the top. Season, toss to mix well, and scatter with a small handful of mint to serve.

Quinoa Salad with Olives, Green Beans, and Feta Cook the quinoa according to the package directions, let cool, and transfer to a wide bowl. Meanwhile, quarter 3 red onions, drizzle with 1 tablespoon olive oil, and roast in a preheated oven, at 425°F, for 12–15 minutes. Blanch 5½ cups halved green beans in a saucepan of boiling water for 3 minutes. Drain, refresh under cold water, and add to the quinoa. Add the roasted red onion, a handful each of finely chopped mint and parsley, 1 cup green olives, and 8 oz feta cheese, crumbled. Season, then drizzle with the juice of 1 orange and ⅓ cup olive oil. Toss to mix well and serve.

Delicatessen Pasta Salad

Serves 4

2 (9 oz) packages fresh spinach
and ricotta tortellini

1 (7 oz) jar mixed sliced roasted
sweet peppers in olive oil

1 (8 oz) jar mushrooms
in olive oil, drained

1 (8 oz) sun-dried tomatoes
in oil, drained

1 cup basil

3 cups arugula

black pepper

- Bring a large saucepan of lightly salted water to a boil. Add the tortellini and cook according to the package directions. Drain well and transfer to a large bowl.

- Add the jar of mixed roasted peppers, including the oil, along with the drained mushrooms and sun-dried tomatoes.

- Add the basil and arugula. Season with black pepper, stir gently to combine, and serve warm.

Italian-Style Pasta Broth

Bring 4 cups vegetable stock to a boil in a large saucepan and add 1 diced carrot, 1 diced onion, and 1 diced celery stick. Bring back to a boil and cook for 10 minutes. Add 2 (9 oz) packages of fresh spinach and ricotta tortellini and cook according to the package directions. Remove from the heat and stir in 1½ cups chopped basil and 1 cup chopped arugula and serve ladled into warm bowls.

Tortellini Pasta Bake

Cook 2 (9 oz) packages fresh spinach and ricotta tortellini according to the package directions, drain, and mix together in a shallow ovenproof dish with 1 (7 oz) jar roasted mixed peppers, 1 (8 oz) jar sun-dried tomatoes, and 1 cup chopped basil. Whisk together 2 eggs, 1 cup heavy cream, and ½ cup grated Parmesan cheese. Season and pour over the tortellini mixture. Bake in a preheated oven, at 400°F, for 15–20 minutes or until bubbling and golden. Serve warm with an arugula salad.

VEG-SOUP-MEC

 Fatoush Salad

Serves 4

1 pita bread, torn into
   small pieces
6 plum tomatoes, seeded
   and coarsely chopped
½ cucumber, peeled and
   coarsely chopped
10 radishes, sliced
1 red onion, coarsely chopped
1 small Boston lettuce,
   leaves separated
small handful of fresh mint

For the dressing

1 cup olive oil
juice of 3 lemons
1 garlic clove, crushed
2 teaspoons sumac
   (or ½ teaspoon ground cumin)
salt and pepper

- First make the dressing. Whisk the olive oil, lemon juice, garlic, and sumac together in a bowl. Season to taste.

- To make the salad, combine the pita pieces, tomatoes, cucumber, radishes, red onion, lettuce leaves, and mint in a large bowl.

- When ready to serve, pour the dressing over the salad and gently mix together to coat the salad evenly.

Middle Eastern Couscous Salad
Replace the pita bread in the above recipe with 2½ cups cooked couscous. Pour over the dressing, toss to mix well, and serve.

Toasted Pita, Hummus, and Salad "Pizzettas" Finely dice 4 plum tomatoes, ½ cucumber, 6 radishes, and ½ red onion and place in a bowl. Add 1 crushed garlic clove, ¼ cup olive oil, 2 teaspoons sumac, and the juice of 1 lemon. Season and stir to mix well. Let stand for 15 minutes. Meanwhile, toast 8 pita breads until lightly golden and place onto 4 serving plates. Spread 2 tablespoons hummus over each one and then top with the prepared salad. Sprinkle over chopped mint and serve.

 # Fruity Potato Salad

Serves 4

8 new potatoes, scrubbed

2 Navel oranges, segmented

2 red apples, such as Red Delicious or Pink Lady, cored and coarsely chopped

⅔ cup green and red seedless grapes

2 celery sticks, thickly sliced

6 scallions, sliced

4 pickles, coarsely chopped

For the dressing

⅓ cup mayonnaise

juice of 1 lemon

1 teaspoon honey

1 tablespoon whole-grain mustard

3 tablespoons each of finely chopped dill and chives

salt and pepper

- First make the dressing. Mix together all the ingredients in a bowl and season to taste.

- Cook the potatoes in boiling salted water for about 15–20 minutes, until just tender. Drain and, when just cool enough to handle, cut into halves or quarters if large.

- Place the potatoes in a mixing bowl with the remaining salad ingredients. Pour the dressing over the salad and toss gently to mix well. Chill the salad until ready to serve.

---

1 **Fruity Pasta Salad** Replace the potatoes in above recipe with 8 oz quick-cooking penne pasta and cook according to the package directions. Place in a bowl with the oranges, apples, grapes, celery, and scallions. Pour over the dressing, toss to mix well, and serve.

 Mustardy Potato and Scallion Gratin Place 12 cooked, sliced new potatoes in a lightly oiled casserole dish or shallow ovenproof dish. Add 6 finely sliced scallions, 2 finely sliced celery sticks, and 2 finely chopped pickles. Toss to mix well. Whisk together

⅔ cup fresh mayonnaise with 2 tablespoons whole-grain mustard, 3 tablespoons each of chopped dill and chives, and 1 egg. Spoon this over the top of the vegetables and place under a preheated medium-hot broiler for 4–5 minutes or until golden and bubbling. Serve immediately.

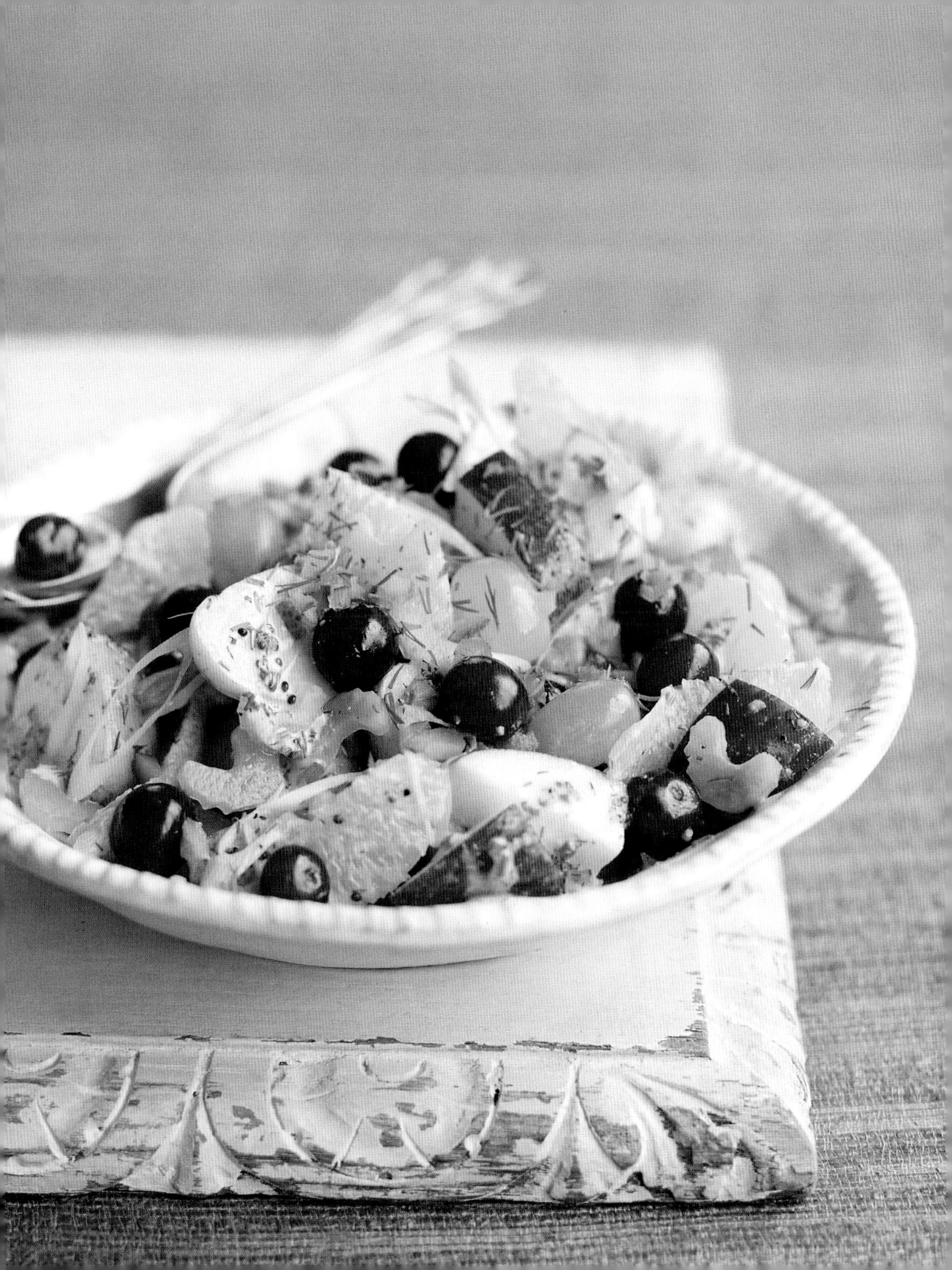

1 Cucumber and Basmati Rice Salad

Serves 4

1 red onion, finely chopped
6 ripe tomatoes, finely chopped
1 cucumber, finely chopped
1 fresh red chile, seeded and
  finely chopped
small handful of finely
  chopped cilantro
small handful of finely
  chopped mint
2 cups basmati rice or other
  long-grain rice, cooked
  and cooled
juice of 2 large limes
2 tablespoons coarsely chopped
  roasted peanuts
salt and pepper

- Put the onion, tomatoes, cucumber, chile, cilantro, mint, and rice in a bowl, and pour over the lime juice.

- Season well, cover, and let stand at room temperature for 5–6 minutes.

- Before serving, stir to mix well and sprinkle over the chopped nuts.

---

2 Linguini with a Fresh Tomato, Chile, and Herb Sauce

Cook 12 oz linguini according to the package directions. Meanwhile, finely chop 1 red onion, 6 plum tomatoes, 1 red chile, and a small handful of cilantro and mint. Place in a bowl with ⅓ cup olive oil, season, and stir to mix well. When the pasta is cooked, drain and divide among 4 serving plates. Top with the pasta sauce and serve immediately.

3 Cheesy Rice and Chile Vegetable Casserole

Place 1 chopped red onion, 6 chopped tomatoes, 1 chopped red chile, and 1½ cups cold, cooked basmati rice or other long-grain rice in a lightly oiled ovenproof dish. Lightly beat 4 eggs in a bowl with 1 teaspoon grated fresh ginger root, 1 teaspoon garlic, 3 tablespoons finely chopped cilantro, and 3 tablespoons finely chopped mint, then season well. Pour the egg mixture into the dish, sprinkle with 2 cups shredded cheddar cheese, and bake in a preheated oven, at 400°F, for 20–25 minutes or until just set and golden. Serve with a crisp green salad.

VEG-SOUP-XOQ

Couscous Salad With Bell Peppers and Preserved Lemon

Serves 4

1 cup couscous

3 cups hot vegetable stock

2 garlic cloves, crushed

½ teaspoon finely grated fresh ginger root

1 teaspoon ground cumin

¼ teaspoon ground cinnamon

1 tablespoon orange zest

½ cup pumpkin seeds

¼ cup olive oil

1 red bell pepper and 1 yellow bell pepper, seeded and finely chopped

4 scallions, finely sliced

6 cherry tomatoes, quartered

1 tablespoon preserved lemon, drained and finely chopped

juice of 1 large orange

2 tablespoons each finely chopped cilantro and mint

- Place the couscous in a saucepan with the stock, garlic, ginger, cumin, cinnamon, and orange zest. Bring to a boil and simmer for 10–12 minutes or until the couscous is tender.

- Meanwhile, toast the pumpkin seeds in a dry skillet.

- Drain the couscous and place in a large mixing bowl with the olive oil, bell peppers, scallions, tomatoes, and preserved lemon.

- Add the orange juice, chopped herbs, and pumpkin seeds. Toss gently to mix well and serve immediately.

10 Vegetable and Couscous Broth

Finely dice 1 red bell pepper and 1 yellow bell pepper and add to a saucepan with 4 sliced scallions, 1 crushed garlic clove, and 5 cups hot vegetable stock. Bring to a boil and cook over high heat for 6–7 minutes. Stir in ⅔ cup cooked couscous and 2 tablespoons each of chopped cilantro and mint. Season and serve immediately.

30 Mixed Bell Pepper Tagine
Heat 3 tablespoons olive oil in a saucepan and add 4 chopped scallions, 2 chopped garlic cloves, 1 teaspoon grated fresh ginger root, 1 teaspoon ground cumin, ¼ teaspoon ground cinnamon, and 2 seeded and chopped bell peppers (1 red and 1 yellow). Stir-fry for 2–3 minutes, then pour in 2 cups hot vegetable stock. Bring to a boil and simmer for 10–12 minutes, then add 1 tablespoon chopped preserved lemon. Mix together 1 tablespoon cornstarch with 2 tablespoons cold water, add to the tagine, stir, and cook until thickened slightly. Remove from the heat and garnish with chopped cilantro before serving with couscous or rice.

VEG-SOUP-KEB

Lentil, Mushroom, and Peppadew Pepper Salad

Serves 4

¼ cup olive oil

4 cups halved or quartered white button mushrooms

2 tablespoons cider vinegar

1 tablespoon Dijon mustard

200 g (7 oz) mild Peppadew peppers or other sweet piquanté peppers, drained and coarsely chopped

6 scallions, finely sliced

1 (15½ oz) can green lentils, drained and rinsed

3 Boston lettuce, leaves separated

4 oz goat cheese

black pepper

- Heat 2 tablespoons of the oil in a nonstick skillet. Add the mushrooms and cook over high heat until just starting to soften.

- Remove from the heat, then stir in the remaining oil with the vinegar and mustard. Stir well until mixed, then add the Peppadew peppers, scallions, and lentils and mix well again.

- Arrange the lettuce leaves over 4 plates. Spoon the lentil salad over them, crumble the goat cheese over the top, and serve sprinkled with freshly ground black pepper.

Lentil and Mushroom Pilaf

Heat 3 tablespoons olive oil in a skillet over high heat. Add 6 chopped scallions and 4 cups sliced mushrooms and stir-fry for 2–3 minutes. Add 4 cups cold, cooked basmati rice or long-grain rice, ¼ cup chopped Peppadew or sweet piquanté peppers, and 1 cup canned, drained green lentils and stir-fry for 3–4 minutes or until piping hot. Remove from the heat and crumble 4 oz goat cheese the top before serving.

Spiced Mushroom and Lentil Curry

Heat 2 tablespoons olive oil in a saucepan and cook 6 chopped scallions, 2 chopped garlic cloves, and 1 teaspoon finely chopped fresh ginger root for 2–3 minutes over low heat. Add 2 teaspoons cumin seeds, 1 teaspoon black mustard seeds, and 2 tablespoons mild curry powder and stir-fry for 1–2 minutes. Stir in 6 cups sliced white button mushrooms and stir-fry over high heat for 3–4 minutes. Add 1 (15½ oz) can green lentils, 1 cup chopped tomatoes, and 1 cup vegetable stock. Bring to a boil and simmer gently for 15–20 minutes. Remove from the heat, stir in ¼ cup crème fraîche or sour cream, season, and serve with rice or warm naan.

 # Insalata Russa or Russian Salad

Serves 4

2 or 3 waxy potatoes, such as
  white rounders or Yellow Finn
2 cooked medium beets
⅔ cup fresh shelled peas
10 baby carrots
½ small cauliflower, broken into
  small florets
1 cup sliced green beans
3 extra-large eggs, hard boiled
6 pickles with dill, finely chopped
⅓ cup mayonnaise
salt and pepper
small bunch of fresh dill,
  to garnish

- Peel the potatoes and chop into ½ inch cubes. Boil in a saucepan of lightly salted water for 10–12 minutes or until tender.

- Chop the beets into cubes about the same size as the potatoes and place in a wide salad bowl.

- Meanwhile blanch the peas, carrots, cauliflower, and beans for 3–4 minutes. Drain and cool.

- Shell and halve the eggs.

- Mix the pickles with the vegetables, then fold the mixture into the mayonnaise in a large bowl. Season and top with the eggs and a few dill sprigs.

---

1 Rainbow Vegetable Sauté

Heat 3 tablespoons olive oil in a large skillet and add 1 chopped onion, 2 cups cooked, diced beet, 1½ cups cooked, diced potatoes, 2 cups cooked, diced carrots, 1⅓ cups peas, and 3 cups trimmed green beans. Stir-fry over high heat for 6–7 minutes, season well, and remove from the heat. Serve with rice or crusty bread.

 2 Creamy Mixed Vegetable Soup

Place ¾ cup finely diced, cooked beets, ⅔ cup finely diced, cooked potatoes, and ⅔ cup finely diced, cooked carrots in a saucepan with 1⅓ cups peas and 2 cups coarsely chopped green beans. Add 3 cups hot vegetable stock and bring to a boil. Cook over high heat for 10 minutes, then stir in 1 cup light cream and ¼ cup finely chopped dill. Season, remove from the heat, and serve.

VEG-SOUP-WUV

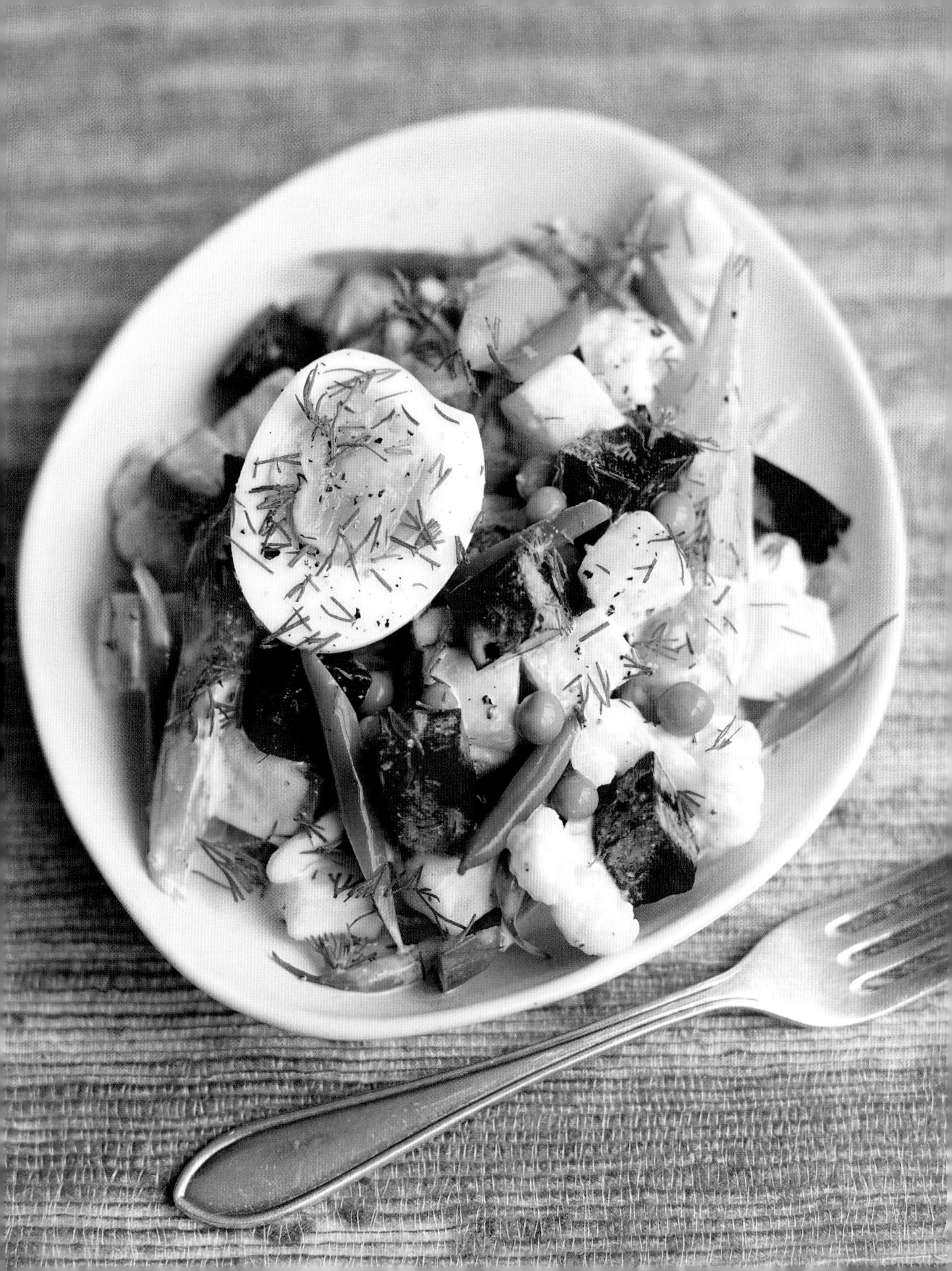

 # Grilled Haloumi, Bell Pepper, and Arugula Salad

Serves 4

24 cherry tomatoes

1 (7 oz) jar mixed sweet peppers in olive oil, drained and sliced

1 (5 oz) package arugula

1 lb haloumi cheese or mozzarella cheese, sliced

For the dressing

grated zest of ½ lemon and 2 tablespoons juice

⅓ cup olive oil

a handful flat leaf parsley, chopped

2 tablespoons small capers, drained and rinsed

black pepper

- First make the dressing. Whisk together the lemon zest and juice, olive oil, parsley, capers, and black pepper, then set aside.

- Halve the tomatoes and divide among 4 plates, along with the sweet peppers and arugula.

- Place the slices of haloumi on a preheated ridged grill pan and place under a preheated medium broiler. Cook for 2–3 minutes on each side until just beginning to warm and soften.

- Transfer the warm haloumi to the plates, drizzle with the dressing, and serve immediately.

---

10 Mediterranean Haloumi Wraps

In a large bowl, mix together 2 tablespoons capers, 2 cups halved cherry tomatoes, 1 (7 oz) jar roasted mixed peppers, chopped, and 2 cups chopped arugula leaves. Squeeze over the juice of 1 lime and season well. Meanwhile, warm 8 oz haloumi cheese or mozzarella cheese, sliced, and 4 large flat-bread wraps in a preheated oven, at 300°F. To serve, divide the vegetable mixture and haloumi among the 4 wraps and fold over to enclose the filling.

 30 Pasta with Haloumi, Arugula, and Cherry Tomatoes

Cut 10 oz haloumi cheese or mozzarella cheese into small bite-size cubes. Heat ¼ cup olive oil in a large skillet. Add the haloumi and stir-fry until lightly golden. Remove from the skillet with a slotted spoon and set aside. Add 2 crushed garlic cloves to the skillet and sauté for 1 minute. Add 2 cups halved cherry tomatoes and 1 finely chopped red chile and cook over low heat for about 10 minutes, until soft. Meanwhile, cook 12 oz short pasta shapes according to the package directions, adding 3 cups arugula leaves during the last minute of cooking. Drain the pasta and add to the cherry tomato mixture in the skillet. Toss to mix well. Top with the drained haloumi, season, and serve.

VEG-SOUP-DYA

Quinoa, Zucchini, and Pomegranate Salad

Serves 4

½ cup quinoa
1 large zucchini
1 tablespoon white wine vinegar
¼ cup olive oil
4 scallions, finely sliced
⅔ cup halved cherry tomatoes
1 red chile, finely chopped
½ cup pomegranate seeds or
   seeds of ½ pomegranate
small handful of finely chopped
   flat leaf parsley
salt and pepper

- Cook the quinoa following the package directions, then drain and rinse under cold water. Drain again.

- Cut the ends off the zucchini, then cut into ribbons using a vegetable peeler.

- Whisk together the vinegar and 2 tablespoons of the oil and season with salt and pepper.

- Put the rest of the ingredients in a large bowl, pour the dressing over the top, toss everything together, and serve.

---

10 Zucchini and Scallion Stir-Fry

Heat 2 tablespoons olive oil in a large wok and add 2 coarsely shredded zucchini, 6 sliced scallions, and ⅔ cup coarsely chopped cherry tomatoes. Stir-fry over high heat for 3–4 minutes. Add ½ cup store-bought stir-fry sauce of your choice and stir-fry for 2–3 minutes, until piping hot. Serve with noodles or rice.

30 Warm Grilled Zucchini and Eggplant Salad with Quinoa

Cook ⅓ cup quinoa according to the package directions. Meanwhile, slice 2 large zucchini and 1 eggplant into ½ inch thick slices, brush with a little olive oil, and cook in a heavy, ridged grill pan over high heat, in batches, for 4–5 minutes on each side, until tender. Place in a wide bowl and scatter with 4 finely sliced scallions, ⅔ cup halved cherry tomatoes, and the cooked quinoa. Mix together ¼ cup olive oil and 1 tablespoon white wine vinegar and sprinkle over the top of the salad. Season, scatter with mint leaves, and serve.

QuickCook

Speedy Midweek Meals

Recipes listed by cooking time

30

2

Quick Roasted Vegetable Pizzas

Serves 4

2 store-bought chilled pizza
crusts (each about 9 inches
in diameter)

1 (14 oz) jar store-bought
pizza sauce

16–20 pitted ripe black olives

1 (12 oz) jar roasted mixed
peppers in olive oil, drained and
coarsely chopped

1 (8 oz) jar sun-dried tomatoes
in oil, drained

3 tablespoons caper berries
or capers

8 marinated artichoke hearts in
oil, drained and quartered

8 oz mozzarella cheese, diced

coarsely chopped parsley or
oregano leaves, to garnish

- Preheat the oven to 425°F.

- Place the pizza crusts on 2 baking sheets.

- Spread the pizza sauce evenly over the pizza crusts
and scatter with the olives, roasted peppers, sun-dried
tomatoes, caper berries, artichoke hearts, and mozzarella.

- Bake in the preheated oven for 12–15 minutes, until golden
and crispy.

- Remove from the oven and garnish with the chopped herbs
before serving.

Mediterranean Roasted Pepper Salad Place 1 (12 oz) jar and 1 (7 oz) jar roasted sweet peppers, drained, in a bowl with 25 pitted black olives, 1 (8 oz) jar sun-dried tomatoes in oil, drained, ¼ cup caper berries or capers, 8 quartered marinated artichoke hearts, and 8 oz mozzarella cheese, sliced. Toss in a handful of arugula and drizzle with ¼ cup of olive oil mixed with the juice of 1 lemon. Season, toss to mix well, and serve.

Warm Mediterranean Rice Salad Place 1⅓ cups long-grain rice in a heavy saucepan with 2 cups vegetable stock. Bring to a boil, cover, and reduce the heat. Cook gently for 15 minutes, then turn off the heat and let stand undisturbed for 10–15 minutes. Meanwhile, place 1 (7 oz) jar roasted peppers, drained, in a wide bowl with ¼ cup pitted ripe black olives, 1 (8 oz) jar sun-dried tomatoes in oil, drained, ¼ cup caper berries or capers, and 8 oz mozzarella, diced. Fluff up the grains of rice with a fork and fold into the vegetables with a small handful of chopped basil. Season, toss to mix well, and serve warm.

30 Black-Eyed Pea and Red Pepper "Stew"

Serves 4

2 tablespoons olive oil

4 shallots, finely chopped

2 garlic cloves, crushed

2 celery sticks, diced

1 large carrot, peeled and cut into ½ inch pieces

1 red bell pepper, seeded and cut into ½ inch pieces

1 teaspoon dried mixed herbs

2 teaspoons ground cumin

1 teaspoon ground cinnamon

2 (14½ oz) cans tomatoes

2 tablespoons tomato paste

⅓ cup vegetable stock

2 (15 oz) cans black-eyed peas in water, drained, or 4 cups cooked dried black-eyed peas

¼ cup finely chopped cilantro, plus extra to garnish

salt and pepper

cooked long-grain rice, to serve

- Heat the oil in a large skillet and place over high heat.

- Add the shallots, garlic, celery, carrot, and red bell pepper and cook for 2–3 minutes or until lightly starting to brown.

- Add the dried herbs, cumin, cinnamon, tomatoes, tomato paste, and stock and bring to a boil. Reduce the heat to medium, cover, and cook gently for 12–15 minutes or until the vegetables are tender, breaking up the tomatoes into small pieces with a wooden spoon toward the end of the cooking time.

- Stir in the black-eyed peas and cook for 2–3 minutes or until piping hot.

- Season well, remove from the heat, and sprinkle over the chopped cilantro. Garnish with cilantro and serve with long-grain rice.

---

10 Colorful Black-Eyed Pea and Vegetable Salad Finely chop 2 carrots, 2 celery sticks, 1 red bell pepper, 2 tomatoes, and 2 shallots and place in a bowl with ¼ cup olive oil and the juice of 2 limes. Season and add 1 (15 oz) can black-eyed peas, drained, and a large handful of chopped cilantro and mint. Toss to mix well and serve with warm flat breads.

20 Hearty Bean and Vegetable Broth Place 1 finely diced carrot, 2 finely diced celery sticks, 2 finely diced shallots, 2 crushed garlic cloves, 2 tablespoons tomato paste, and 2 teaspoons dried mixed herbs in a heavy saucepan with 4 cups hot vegetable stock and bring to a boil. Cook, uncovered, over medium heat for 10–12 minutes. Stir in 2 (15 oz) cans black-eyed peas, drained, and bring back to a boil. Season, remove from the heat, and serve ladled into warm bowls with crusty bread.

Creamy Zucchini Orzo Pasta

Serves 4

12 oz dried orzo
  (rice-shaped pasta)
1 tablespoon butter
1 tablespoon olive oil
1 red chile, seeded and
  finely chopped
2 garlic cloves, finely chopped
4 scallions, finely chopped
3 medium zucchini,
  coarsely shredded
finely grated zest of 1 small
  unwaxed lemon
⅔ cup cream cheese with
  garlic and herbs
¼ cup finely chopped
  flat leaf parsley
salt and pepper

· Bring a large saucepan of lightly salted water to a boil, then cook the pasta according to the package directions.

· Meanwhile, heat the butter and olive oil in a large skillet, then add the chile, garlic, scallions, and zucchini. Cook over medium-low heat for 10–15 minutes, or until softened, stirring often.

· Reduce the heat and add the lemon zest. Cook gently for 3–4 minutes, add the cream cheese, and mix thoroughly. Season to taste.

· Drain the pasta and add to the zucchini mixture. Stir in the parsley, mix well, and serve immediately.

---

10 Stir-Fried Zucchini with Scallions and Chile Heat 2 tablespoons olive oil in a large skillet. Add 6 sliced scallions, 2 crushed garlic cloves, 1 chopped red chile, and 3 coarsely shredded zucchini. Stir-fry over high heat for 4–5 minutes and then add 1¼ lb quick-cooking, stir-fry rice noodles and ¼ cup light soy sauce. Toss to mix well and stir-fry for 2–3 minutes or until piping hot. Serve immediately.

20 Minted Zucchini, Cherry Tomato, and Orzo Pasta Salad Cook 12 oz orzo pasta according to the package directions. Meanwhile, place 2 coarsely shredded zucchini, 4 sliced scallions, ¼ cup finely chopped mint, and 1⅓ cups halved cherry tomatoes in a wide salad bowl. Make a dressing by whisking together 1 finely chopped red chile, 2 crushed garlic cloves, ⅓ cup olive oil, the juice of 1 lemon, and 1 teaspoon honey. Season well. Drain the pasta and rinse under cold running water until cool. Drain again and add to the salad bowl. Pour over the dressing and toss to mix well before serving.

VEG-SPEE-WUV

Greek-Style Summer Omelet

Serves 4

8 extra-large eggs
1 teaspoon dried oregano
1 tablespoon finely chopped mint
¼ cup finely chopped
  flat leaf parsley
2 tablespoons olive oil
2 small red onions, peeled and
  coarsely chopped
2 large ripe tomatoes, coarsely
  chopped
½ zucchini, coarsely chopped
1 cup pitted ripe black olives
4 oz feta cheese
salt and pepper
crisp green salad, to serve
  (optional)

- Whisk the eggs in a bowl and add the oregano, mint, and parsley. Season well.

- Heat the oil in a large nonstick skillet. Add the red onion and cook over high heat for about 3–4 minutes or until brown around the edges.

- Add the tomatoes, zucchini, and olives and cook for 3–4 minutes or until the vegetables begin to soften.

- Meanwhile, preheat the broiler to medium-high.

- Reduce the heat to medium and pour the eggs into the skillet. Cook, stirring as they begin to set, for 3–4 minutes, until they are firm but still slightly runny in places.

- Scatter with the feta, then place the skillet under the preheated broiler for 4–5 minutes or until the omelet is puffed up and golden.

- Cut into wedges and serve with a crisp green salad, if liked.

---

1 Classic Greek Salad

Thinly slice 2 red onions, 4 tomatoes, and 1 cucumber and place in a wide salad bowl with 8 oz feta cheese, cubed, and 1 cup pitted ripe black olives. Drizzle ⅓ cup of olive oil over the top and sprinkle with 1 teaspoon dried oregano. Season, toss to mix well, and serve.

2 Warm Greek-Style Pasta Salad

Cook 8 oz short pasta shapes according to the package directions. Meanwhile, coarsely chopped 2 small red onions, 1 cup pitted ripe black olives, 4 tomatoes, and ½ cucumber and place in a salad bowl with a handful of chopped mint. Make a dressing by whisking together 1 crushed garlic clove, ⅓ cup olive oil, 2 tablespoons vinegar, 1 teaspoon mustard, and 1 teaspoon dried oregano, then season. Drain the pasta and add to the salad with the dressing. Toss to mix well and serve warm.

Beet Pasta with Herbs

Serves 4

12 oz quick-cooking pasta
8 cooked beets
1 cup crème fraîche
  or sour cream
¼ cup chopped chives
¼ cup chopped dill
salt and pepper

· Cook the pasta according to the package directions.

· Meanwhile, finely dice the beet and add to the pasta for the last minute of the cooking time.

· Drain the pasta and beets and return to the saucepan. Stir in the crème fraîche and herbs.

· Season and serve immediately.

Speedy Beet and Herb "Risotto"

Blend 2 cups coarsely chopped cooked beets with ⅓ cup heavy cream and ½ cup vegetable stock in a food processor until smooth. Stir-fry 1 crushed garlic clove and 1 finely chopped onion in a skillet with 3 tablespoons olive oil for 3–4 minutes, until softened. Add the beet mixture and 4 cups cold, cooked long-grain rice and stir-fry over high heat for 4–5 minutes or until piping hot. Season with salt and pepper and stir in a small handful each of chopped chives and dill. Serve with a dollop of crème fraîche or sour cream, diced beets, and chopped dill.

Spiced Beet Pilaf

Heat 2 tablespoons of oil with 2 tablespoons butter in a heavy saucepan over medium heat and sauté 2 chopped shallots and 1 chopped garlic clove for 1–2 minutes. Add 1 cinnamon stick, 3 teaspoons cumin seeds, 1 teaspoon curry powder, 1 teaspoon crushed coriander seeds, 2 cups quick-cooking long-grain rice, 2 cups finely diced cooked beets, and 1 finely diced carrot and stir to mix well. Add 4 cups hot vegetable stock, season well, and bring to a boil. Cover tightly and reduce the heat to low. Cook for 10–12 minutes without lifting the lid. Remove from the heat and let stand, undisturbed, for 10 minutes. Remove the lid, fluff up the rice grains with a fork, and serve.

30 Green Vegetable Curry

Serves 4

1 tablespoon sunflower oil

3 tablespoons Thai green curry paste

2 red chiles (optional)

1 (14 fl oz) can coconut milk

1 cup vegetable stock

6 kaffir lime leaves or 1 tablespoon finely grated lime zest

2 tablespoons soy sauce

1 tablespoon brown sugar

3 carrots

¼ butternut squash

1½ cups sugarsnap peas

⅔ cup finely chopped cilantro

juice of 1 lime

steamed jasmine rice, to serve

- Seed and finely slice the chiles, if using. Peel the carrots and cut into thick sticks. Peel and seed the butternut squash, then cut the flesh into ¾ inch cubes.

- Heat the oil in a large nonstick wok or saucepan. Add the curry paste and chiles, if using, and stir-fry for 2–3 minutes.

- Stir in the coconut milk, stock, lime leaves or lime zest, soy sauce, sugar, carrots, and butternut squash. Simmer, uncovered, for 6–8 minutes, stirring occasionally.

- Add the sugarsnaps and continue to simmer for 4–5 minutes.

- Remove from the heat and stir in the cilantro and lime juice.

- Serve ladled into warm bowls accompanied by steamed jasmine rice.

---

10 Mild Thai Green Vegetable Soup

Place 1 tablespoon Thai green curry paste in a saucepan with 1 (14 fl oz) can coconut milk and 1¼ cups vegetable stock. Bring to a boil and add 3 cups sugarsnap peas, 1⅓ cups peas, and 2⅔ cups corn kernels. Cook for 5–6 minutes, then remove from the heat and stir in ⅓ cup chopped cilantro and squeeze over the juice of 1 lime. Serve immediately.

20 Thai Green Vegetable Rice

Heat 1 tablespoon sunflower oil in a large wok or skillet and add 2 sliced shallots, 1⅓ cups finely diced carrots, 1½ cups finely diced butternut squash, and 2 cups sliced sugarsnap peas. Stir-fry over high heat for 4–5 minutes, then add 2 tablespoons Thai green curry paste and 1 cup coconut milk. Stir and cook over high heat for 4–5 minutes, then add 4 cups cold, cooked jasmine rice or other long-grain rice. Stir and cook for 3–4 minutes or until well mixed and piping hot. Scatter over a small handful of chopped cilantro, season, and serve.

VEG-SPEE-HAY

 # Rustic Italian-Style Mushrooms with Cornmeal

Serves 4

1 cup cornmeal or polenta

1 tablespoon finely chopped rosemary

1 tablespoon finely chopped sage

½ cup finely chopped flat leaf parsley

¼ lb (1 stick) butter

6½ cups hot vegetable stock

1½ lb large portobello mushrooms, thickly sliced

3 garlic cloves, crushed

½ cup cream cheese with garlic and herbs

½ teaspoon crushed red pepper

salt and pepper

- Place the cornmeal, rosemary, sage, half the parsley, and half the butter in a saucepan over medium heat and gradually beat in the stock, stirring continuously.

- Reduce the heat to low, season well, and stir continuously until the cornmeal becomes thick and starts bubbling (this will take about 6–8 minutes). Remove from the heat and keep warm.

- Meanwhile, heat the remaining butter in a large nonstick skillet over high heat. Add the mushrooms and garlic and cook for 6–8 minutes. Season well and stir in the cream cheese and crushed red pepper. Cook for 2–3 minutes, until bubbling. Remove from the heat and stir in the remaining parsley.

- Serve immediately on warm plates over the cornmeal.

Creamy Mushroom and Herb Pasta

Cook 12 oz quick-cook pasta according to the package directions. Meanwhile, heat a large skillet over high heat and add 2 tablespoons butter, 2 finely chopped garlic cloves, and 1½ lb thinly sliced portobello mushrooms. Cook over high heat for 3–4 minutes, then stir in 1 cup cream cheese with garlic and herbs. Season, toss to mix well, and stir in 3 tablespoons chopped parsley. Serve over the pasta.

Mixed Mushrooms on Polenta

Cut a 1 lb roll of polenta (precooked, hard-set Italian-style polenta) into thick slices and set aside. Heat 3 tablespoons butter in a large skillet. Add 1½ lb mixed sliced mushrooms and 1 tablespoon thyme. Season well and cook for 6–8 minutes. Increase the heat and add 2 chopped garlic cloves. Cook for 30 seconds, then pour in ¼ cup red wine and cook for another 2 minutes. Meanwhile broil the polenta slices under a preheated medium broiler for 1–2 minutes on each side. Divide among 4 serving plates. Top with the mushrooms and a dollop of crème fraîche or Greek yogurt and serve.

VEG-SPEE-RAN

Herbed Quinoa Taboulleh with Olives and Cucumber

Serves 4

1 cucumber, peeled, halved, seeded, and thinly sliced

1 red onion, thinly sliced

juice of 1 lemon

juice of ½ an orange

1 cup quinoa

2½ cups vegetable stock

1 tablespoon olive oil

¼ cup each of chopped cilantro, mint, and parsley

1 cup pitted green olives

¼ (14 oz) jar Peppadew peppers or other piquanté peppers, drained and coarsely chopped

salt and pepper

- Place the cucumber and red onion in a bowl, season well, and pour the lemon and orange juices over the top. Cover and set aside.

- Rinse the quinoa thoroughly under cold water in a strainer. Drain and place in a heavy saucepan over medium heat. Cook, stirring continuously, for 3–4 minutes or until the grains separate and begin to brown.

- Add the stock and bring to a boil, stirring continuously. Reduce the heat and cook for 15 minutes or until the liquid is absorbed. Transfer to a wide serving bowl and drizzle with the olive oil.

- Spoon the cucumber and red onion mixture with its juices over the top and stir in the chopped herbs, olives, and Peppadew peppers.

- Check the seasoning, toss to mix well, and serve.

1 **Herbed Rice Salad** Replace the quinoa in the recipe above with 2 cups cooked and cooled instant rice. In addition, stir in 2 cups bean sprouts and 12 sliced radishes to the cucumber mixture. Toss to mix well and serve.

2 **Herbed Cucumber and Olive Soup with Quinoa** Place 4 cups hot vegetable stock in a saucepan with 2 finely diced cucumbers, 1 cup chopped green olives, and ¼ (14 oz) jar Peppadew peppers, drained and chopped. Boil, uncovered, for 12–15 minutes, then stir in ¼ cup of cooked quinoa. Season and serve immediately.

Spinach, Cherry Tomato, and Blue Cheese Pasta Salad

Serves 4

12 oz macaroni or other short pasta shapes, cooked and cooled
2 cups baby spinach
2⅔ cups halved cherry tomatoes
4 sliced scallions
1 cup store-bought blue cheese dressing
salt and pepper

- Place the cooked and cooled macaroni in a salad bowl with the spinach, cherry tomatoes and scallions.
- Drizzle the blue cheese dressing over the top.
- Season to taste, toss to mix well, and serve immediately.

Cheesy Spinach and Tomato Pasta

Cook 12 oz macaroni according to the package directions. Meanwhile, heat 1½ cups store-bought fresh cheese sauce according to the package directions and pour into a large saucepan with 2 cups halved cherry tomatoes and 3½ cups baby spinach. Stir to mix well and cook over low heat or until the spinach has wilted. Toss in the drained pasta, season, and serve immediately.

Macaroni and Cheese with Spinach and Tomatoes

Cook 8 oz macaroni in a large saucepan of boiling salted water for 8–10 minutes, drain well, and set aside. Meanwhile, melt 3 tablespoons butter over medium heat in a heavy saucepan. Add ⅓ cup all-purpose flour and stir to form a roux, cooking for a few minutes. Warm 2½ cups milk separately. Whisk in the warm milk, a little at a time. Cook for 10–15 minutes, until the sauce is thick and smooth. Stir in 3½ cups finely chopped baby spinach and ⅔ cup cherry tomatoes and season well. Remove from the heat, add 1¾ cups shredded cheddar cheese, and stir until the cheese is well combined and melted. Add the macaroni and mix well. Transfer to a deep ovenproof dish. Sprinkle with ½ cup shredded cheddar cheese and place under a preheated hot broiler. Cook until the cheese is browned and bubbling. Serve immediately.

Mixed Beans and Rice with Eggs

Serves 4

4 eggs
2 tablespoons olive oil
1 onion, chopped
2 tablespoons mild curry powder
1⅓ cups long grain rice
3 cups vegetable stock
3 cups mixed canned beans,
   such as red kidney beans,
   chickpeas, and pinto beans,
   drained and rinsed
⅔ cup sour cream

To garnish

2 tomatoes, finely chopped
3 tablespoons chopped
   fresh herbs

- Hard boil the eggs, then plunge into cold water to cool. Shell, cut into wedges, and set aside.

- Meanwhile, heat the oil and cook the onion for about 3–4 minutes, until soft.

- Stir in the curry powder and rice, then add the stock. Bring to a boil, cover, and simmer for 10–15 minutes, until the rice is cooked.

- Stir through the beans and sour cream. Season to taste and serve topped with the eggs and garnished with the tomatoes and herbs.

10 **Mixed Bean, Tomato, and Rice Salad** Place 3 cups mixed canned beans, such as red kidney beans, chickpeas, and pinto beans, in a wide bowl with 4 chopped tomatoes, 1 chopped red onion, ¼ cup chopped dill, and 2 cups cooked long-grain rice. Mix 1 teaspoon mild curry powder with 1 cup store-bought French salad dressing, pour over the top of salad, toss to mix well, and serve.

 20 **Spiced Bean and Rice Broth** Heat 1 tablespoon olive oil in a saucepan and add 1 chopped onion and 1 tablespoon curry powder, then cook for 1–2 minutes. Stir in 4 cups hot vegetable stock, 3 cups mixed canned beans, such as kidney beans, chickpeas, and pinto beans, 2 chopped tomatoes, and ⅓ cup long-grain rice. Bring to a boil and cook, uncovered, for 15 minutes or until the rice is tender. Season, stir in ¼ cup chopped cilantro, and serve ladled into warm bowls.

 # Kale and Pecorino Pesto Linguini

Serves 4

12 oz linguini
10 oz kale
2 tablespoons olive oil
3 garlic cloves, crushed
¾ cup pine nuts, toasted
4 oz mascarpone cheese
1 cup grated pecorino cheese,
    plus extra shavings to garnish
½ teaspoon grated nutmeg
salt and pepper

- Cook the pasta according to the package directions.

- Meanwhile, wash the kale well, remove any tough stems, and coarsely chop.

- Heat the oil in a saucepan and sauté the garlic for 2–3 minutes. Add the kale to the pan, cover, and cook for 2–3 minutes, or until the kale starts to wilt.

- Place the pine nuts into a food processor or blender and process until smooth. Add the mascarpone, pecorino, and nutmeg. Process again.

- Add the kale and garlic mixture and process until smooth. Season to taste.

- Drain the pasta and return it to the pan. Add the pesto and toss to mix well. Serve garnished with shavings of pecorino.

1 Tomato and Pesto Soup

Heat 4 cups cream of tomato soup until piping hot and ladle into shallow soup plates. Swirl ¼ cup Kale and Pecorino pesto (from the recipe above) into each serving, scatter 3 cups store-bought croutons over the top, and serve immediately.

2 Kale and Pecorino Pasta Frittata

Mix together 12 oz linguini, cooked and drained, with 4 beaten eggs and ⅔ cup Kale and Pecorino Pesto (from the recipe above). Season well. Preheat the broiler to medium-high. Heat 2 tablespoons olive oil in a large skillet and add the pasta mixture. Flatten the mixture with a spoon and cook over medium heat for 8–10 minutes, then place under the preheated broiler for 4–5 minutes or until golden. Serve immediately with a crisp green salad.

 Mixed Bean and Tomato Chili

Serves 4

2 tablespoons olive oil
1 onion, finely chopped
4 garlic cloves, crushed
1 teaspoon dried red chile
2 teaspoons ground cumin
1 teaspoon cinnamon
1 (14½ oz) can diced tomatoes
1½ cups mixed canned beans,
   such as pinto beans and black
   beans, rinsed and drained
1 (15 oz) can red kidney beans
   in chili sauce
salt and pepper

To serve

¼ cup sour cream
1 cup finely chopped cilantro,
   to garnish
grilled corn tortillas

- Heat the oil in a heavy saucepan and add the onion and garlic. Stir-fry for 3–4 minutes, then add the chile, cumin, and cinnamon.

- Stir-fry for 2–3 minutes, then stir in the tomatoes. Bring the mixture to a boil, reduce the heat to medium, and simmer gently for 10 minutes.

- Stir in the beans and cook for 3–4 minutes, until warmed through. Season well and served ladled into 4 warm bowls.

- Top each serving with a tablespoon of sour cream, garnish with chopped cilantro, and serve immediately with corn tortillas.

 Mixed Bean Chili Bruschettas Place
½ onion in a food processor with 2 crushed garlic cloves, 1 teaspoon crushed red pepper, ⅔ cup chopped tomatoes, 1¾ cups mixed canned beans, such as red kidney beans, black beans, and pinto beans, rinsed and drained, and ¼ cup chopped flat leaf parsley. Process until fairly smooth, season, and spread the mixture onto toasted ciabatta or sliced sourdough bread, drizzle with a little olive oil, and serve.

Mexican Tortilla Casserole Place
the chili mixture from the recipe above into a lightly greased, medium ovenproof dish. Layer the top with 7 oz tortilla chips. Whisk together 1 cup sour cream with 3 eggs and pour over the tortilla chip layer. Sprinkle over 1 cup shredded cheddar cheese and bake in a preheated oven, at 425°F, for 15 minutes or until bubbling and lightly golden. Serve warm or at room temperature.

Pasta with Asparagus, Beans, and Pesto

Serves 4

12 oz short pasta shapes
8 oz asparagus tips, halved
2 cups halved green beans
2 tablespoons olive oil
2 tablespoons fresh or store-
   bought bread crumbs
⅓ cup crème fraîche
   or sour cream
⅓ cup store-bought pesto
¼ cup grated Parmesan cheese
salt and pepper

· Bring a large saucepan of salted water to a boil. Add the pasta and cook according to the package directions, adding the asparagus and beans for the last 2 minutes of the cooking time.

· Heat the oil in a small skillet and cook the bread crumbs with a pinch of salt until golden.

· Drain the pasta and vegetables, then return to the pan along with the crème fraîche, pesto, and a generous grinding of pepper.

· Serve in warm bowls, scattered with the crispy bread crumbs and freshly grated Parmesan.

Asparagus, Pesto, and Potato Salad

Place 12 oz blanched asparagus tips in a bowl with 8 boiled and halved baby new potatoes and 2 cups halved cherry tomatoes. Mix together 1 cup crème fraîche or sour cream with ⅓ cup store-bought pesto, season, and pour over the salad mixture. Toss to mix well and serve.

Asparagus and Green Bean Risotto with Pesto Heat 2 tablespoons olive oil and 2 tablespoons butter in a heavy saucepan. When the butter is foaming, add 1 chopped onion and 2 chopped garlic cloves and cook for 2–3 minutes, until beginning to soften. Add 2 cups risotto rice, 8 oz asparagus tips, and 2 cups halved green beans. Stir well and cook for

1–2 minutes, then add ⅔ cup dry white wine and simmer for 1 minute, stirring continuously. Reduce the heat and ladle in 5 cups hot vegetable stock, 1 ladleful at a time, stirring continuously, until each amount is absorbed and the rice is creamy but still firm to the bite. Remove from the heat and stir in ½ cup grated Parmesan and ¼ cup of fresh pesto. Season well and serve immediately.

Ranch-Style Eggs

Serves 4

2 tablespoons olive oil

1 onion, finely sliced

1 red chile, seeded and finely chopped

1 garlic clove, crushed

1 teaspoon ground cumin

1 teaspoon dried oregano

1 (14 oz) can cherry tomatoes

1 (7 oz) jar roasted peppers in oil, drained and coarsely chopped

4 eggs

salt and pepper

¼ cup finely chopped cilantro, to garnish

- Heat the oil in a large skillet and add the onion, chile, garlic, cumin, and oregano.

- Cook gently for about 5 minutes or until soft, then add the tomatoes and roasted peppers and cook for another 5 minutes. If the sauce looks dry, add a splash of water.

- Season well and make 4 hollows in the mixture, break an egg into each, and cover the skillet. Cook for 5 minutes or until the eggs are just set.

- Serve immediately, garnished with chopped cilantro.

---

10 Spicy Mexican-Style Scrambled Eggs Heat 1 tablespoon each olive oil and butter in a large skillet. Whisk together 8 eggs with 1 crushed garlic clove, 1 finely chopped red chile, 1 teaspoon dried oregano, and 1 teaspoon ground cumin. Season, pour into the skillet, and cook over medium-low heat, stirring often, until the eggs are scrambled and cooked to your liking. Serve with warm tortillas and garnish with chopped cilantro.

20 Mexican-Style Sauce Heat 2 tablespoons olive oil in a large skillet and add 1 finely chopped onion, 1 finely chopped red chile, 1 teaspoon each of ground cumin and dried oregano, 2 (14 oz) cans cherry tomatoes, and 1 (7 oz) jar roasted red peppers in oil, drained and chopped. Season, bring to a boil, and cook over medium heat for 12–15 minutes. Stir in a small handful of chopped cilantro and serve over cooked pasta or rice.

30 Rigatoni with Fresh Tomato, Chile, Garlic, and Basil

Serves 4

6 large, ripe plum tomatoes
1 tablespoon extra-virgin olive oil
2 cloves of garlic, finely diced
1 red chile, seeded and
   finely diced
1/3 cup vegetable stock
2/3 cup finely chopped fresh basil
12 oz dried rigatoni
grated Parmesan cheese,
   to serve (optional)
salt and pepper

- Place the tomatoes in a bowl and pour over boiling water to cover. Let stand for 1–2 minutes, then drain, cut across the stem end of each tomato, and peel off the skins.

- When cool enough to handle, cut the tomatoes in half horizontally and shake or gently spoon out the seeds and finely dice the flesh.

- Heat the oil in a large, nonstick skillet and add the garlic and chile. Cook on medium-low heat for 1–2 minutes or until the garlic is fragrant but not browned.

- Add the tomatoes, stock, and basil, season well, and cook gently, stirring often, for 6–8 minutes or until thickened.

- Meanwhile, cook the rigatoni according to the package directions, drain, and toss into the tomato sauce mixture.

- Spoon into warm bowls and serve with grated Parmesan, if liked.

10 No-Cook Fresh Tomato, Chile, and Basil Sauce Finely chop 6 ripe plum tomatoes and place in a bowl with 2 crushed garlic cloves, 1 finely chopped red chile, and 1¼ cups finely chopped basil. Pour over ½ cup extra virgin olive oil and season well. Serve over cooked pasta, couscous, or rice.

20 Tomato, Chile, and Mozzarella Pasta Casserole Preheat the oven to 425°F. Place 1 lb rigatoni, cooked and drained, in a shallow ovenproof dish and spoon over 1 (24 oz) jar of store-bought tomato and basil sauce. Season, add a finely chopped red chile, toss to mix well, then top with 12 oz sliced mozzarella cheese. Bake for 15–20 minutes or until golden and bubbling. Serve immediately.

VEG-SPEE-RUK

30 Spinach Lentils with Cherry Tomatoes

Serves 4

1½ cups dried red split lentils
1 cup coconut milk
2½ cups vegetable stock
1 teaspoon each ground cumin,
    ground coriander, turmeric,
    ground ginger
1 (10 oz) package spinach, chopped
1¼ cups cherry tomatoes
¼ teaspoon garam masala
½ cup finely chopped cilantro
    leaves and stems
salt and pepper
naan or rice, to serve

For the tarka

2 tablespoons sunflower oil
4 shallots, thinly sliced
3 garlic cloves, thinly sliced
1 teaspoon finely chopped ginger
¼ teaspoon chili powder
2 teaspoons cumin seeds
1 teaspoon black mustard seeds

- Place the lentils in a strainer and rinse under cold running water until the water runs clear. Drain and transfer to a wide saucepan with the coconut milk, stock, cumin, coriander, turmeric, and ginger. Bring the mixture to a boil, skimming off any scum as it rises to the surface, then cover. Reduce the heat and simmer for 15–20 minutes, stirring occasionally to prevent the mixture from sticking to the bottom of the saucepan.

- Stir in the spinach and cherry tomatoes and cook for 6–8 minutes, or until the lentils are soft and tender, adding a little stock or water if the mixture seems too thick.

- Meanwhile, make the "tarka." Heat the oil in a small skillet and sauté the shallots, garlic, ginger, chili powder, and cumin and mustard seeds, stirring often. Cook for 3–4 minutes, until the shallots are lightly browned, then transfer this mixture to the cooked lentils.

- Stir in the garam masala and chopped cilantro, then check the seasoning. Serve with naan or rice.

---

10 Lentil, Tomato, and Spinach Soup

Heat 4 cups canned lentil soup in a large saucepan with 1 (6 oz) package baby spinach, 1 tablespoon mild curry powder, and 1¼ cups halved cherry tomatoes. Bring to a boil and simmer for 2–3 minutes, until piping hot. Serve ladled into bowls and topped with a dollop of plain yogurt.

20 Spicy Cherry Tomato and Spinach Curry

Process 2 tablespoons each of grated fresh ginger root and garlic with 3 plum tomatoes in a blender. Heat ½ cup sunflower oil in a large skillet, add 2¾ cups cherry tomatoes, and cook for 1–2 minutes. Remove with a slotted spoon and drain on paper towels. Pour 1 tablespoon oil into the skillet and add 2 teaspoons each of fennel and nigella seeds. Cook for 1–2 minutes, then add the ginger, garlic, and tomato mixture with 3 cups chopped spinach. Cook until the spinach is wilted, then add 1 teaspoon each of ground coriander, turmeric, and paprika. Season well. Add the cherry tomatoes and cook over medium heat, stirring often, for 6–8 minutes, until smooth and thick. Serve with naan or chapattis.

3 Cauliflower and Cheese

Serves 4

8 baby cauliflowers, trimmed, or
  1 medium head of cauliflower,
  cut into large florets
2½ tablespoons butter, plus extra
  for greasing
2 cups whole milk
⅓ cup all-purpose flour
2 bay leaves
pinch of freshly grated nutmeg
3 cups shredded sharp cheddar
  cheese
¼ cup grated Parmesan cheese
salt and pepper

- Lightly butter a shallow, ovenproof dish.

- To make the sauce, melt the butter in a heavy saucepan. Gently heat the milk in a separate saucepan. Stir the flour into the melted butter and cook on low heat for 2–3 minutes, stirring from time to time. Remove the pan from the heat and pour in a little of the warm milk, stirring continuously. Gradually add the rest of the milk, again stirring continuously. Add the bay leaves and nutmeg and season well. Return the pan to low heat and cook for 10–12 minutes (or until there is no taste of flour), stirring frequently. Stir in the cheddar, remove from the heat, and remove and discard the bay leaves.

- Preheat the broiler to medium-high.

- Meanwhile, cook the baby cauliflowers or cauliflower florets in boiling water for about 5–6 minutes. Drain well, then place in the prepared dish and pour over the sauce.

- Sprinkle over the Parmesan and cook under a preheated broiler for 1 minute, until lightly browned. Serve immediately.

---

1 Easy Cauliflower and Mustard Cheese

Heat 1½ cups store-bought white sauce according to the package directions with ¼ cup shredded cheddar cheese. Meanwhile, blanch the florets from 1 large head of cauliflower for 5–6 minutes, until just tender, and place in a serving bowl. Mix 2 tablespoons Dijon mustard with the sauce and pour over the florets. Season, toss to mix well, and serve with crusty bread.

2 Creamy Cauliflower Soup

Place the florets from 1 medium head of cauliflower, 1 chopped onion, and 1 crushed garlic clove in a saucepan with 4 cups hot vegetable stock. Bring to a boil, cover, and cook over medium heat for 12–15 minutes. Add 1¼ cups heavy cream and bring back to a boil. Remove from the heat and process, using an immersion blender, until smooth. Season and stir in 2 cups shredded cheddar cheese just before serving.

Stir-Fried Vegetable Rice

Serves 4

2 tablespoons sunflower oil

6 scallions, cut diagonally into
1 inch lengths

2 garlic cloves, crushed

1 teaspoon finely grated fresh
ginger root

1 red bell pepper, seeded and
finely chopped

1 carrot, peeled and finely diced

2 cups peas

4 cups cooked, white
long-grain rice

1 tablespoon dark soy sauce

1 tablespoon sweet chili sauce

chopped cilantro and mint,
to garnish

- Heat the oil in a large, nonstick wok and add the scallions, garlic, and ginger. Stir-fry for 4–5 minutes, then add the red bell pepper, carrot, and peas. Stir-fry over high heat for 3–4 minutes.

- Stir in the rice, soy sauce, and sweet chili sauce and stir-fry for 3–4 minutes or until the rice is heated through and piping hot.

- Remove from the heat and serve immediately, garnished with the chopped herbs.

Veggie Noodle Stir-Fry

Heat 2 tablespoons oil in a wok and add 1 (12 oz) package of prepared stir-fry vegetables. Stir-fry for 2–3 minutes over high heat, then add 1¼ lb fresh egg noodles and ½ cup store-bought stir-fry sauce. Stir-fry for 1–2 minutes or until piping hot and serve immediately.

 Chinese Vegetables, Szechuan Style Heat 2 tablespoons vegetable oil in a wok or deep skillet and add 3 chopped shallots, 2 thinly sliced chiles, 2 teaspoons each of grated fresh ginger root and garlic, 1 teaspoon crushed Szechuan peppercorns, and a pinch of salt. Stir-fry for 1 minute, add 5 oz firm tofu, diced, and stir-fry for another 2 minutes, then remove to a plate. Cut 1 carrot into thin sticks and 2 red bell peppers into thin strips. Halve 3 cups snow peas lengthwise. Heat 2 tablespoons sunflower oil and stir-fry the vegetables until starting to wilt, then add ¼ cup light soy sauce and 2 tablespoons Chinese rice wine. Return the tofu and flavorings to the wok or pan and toss everything together. Drizzle with 1 tablespoon sesame oil and serve with cooked egg noodles or store-bought fried rice.

 # Tomato and Eggplant Pappardelle

Serves 4

¼ cup extra virgin olive oil

1 large eggplant, cut into
   ¾ inch dice

1 small onion, finely diced

2 garlic cloves, crushed

1½ cups store-bought tomato
   and basil pasta sauce

12 oz dried pappardelle
   or tagliatelle

8 oz mozzarella cheese, drained
   and diced

To garnish

¼ cup grated Parmesan cheese
   (optional)

basil, to garnish (optional)

- Bring a large saucepan of salted water to a boil.

- Meanwhile, heat the oil in a large skillet over medium-high heat. Add the eggplant and onion and cook, stirring, for 5 minutes.

- Add the garlic and cook for 1 minute. Add the tomato sauce and 1 cup water to the skillet, bring to a simmer, and cook for 8–10 minutes, or until the eggplants are just tender. Season to taste.

- Cook the pasta in the saucepan of boiling water according to the package directions. Remove from the heat, drain, and return to the pan.

- Stir the mozzarella into the sauce until it begins to melt and become stringy, then add to the pasta. Toss to mix well, sprinkle with the Parmesan, and garnish with basil, if liked.

 Tomato, Eggplant, and Mozzarella Pizzas Preheat the oven to 425°F. Place 2 store-bought pizza crusts on 2 baking sheets and spread over the tomato and eggplant sauce from the above recipe. Scatter with 8 oz mozzarella, diced, and place in the oven for 8–10 minutes. Serve immediately.

 Grilled Eggplant, Tomato, and Basil Salad Thinly slice 2 large eggplants and brush with olive oil. Cook in a preheated heavy, ridged grill pan over high heat for 2–3 minutes on each side or until tender. Transfer to a platter with 4 large, sliced tomatoes and 8 oz sliced mozzarella cheese. Whisk together ⅓ cup olive oil with 1 crushed garlic clove and the juice of 1 lemon. Season and drizzle over the top of the salad. Scatter over a handful of basil and serve.

Tex-Mex Corn Salad

Serves 4

2½ cups corn kernels

1 (12 oz) jar roasted red peppers, drained and sliced

1 finely chopped red onion

¼ cup chopped jalapeno peppers (from a jar)

1 (15 oz) can red kidney beans, drained

¼ cup chopped parsley

⅓ cup store-bought salad dressing

salt and pepper

- Place the corn kernels in a bowl with the roasted peppers, onion, jalapeno peppers, and kidney beans. Scatter withe the chopped parsley.

- Drizzle the salad dressing over the salad, season, toss to mix well, and serve immediately.

20 Corn, Red Pepper, and Potato Hash

Bring a saucepan of salted water to a boil and cook 2½ cups diced potatoes for 5 minutes. Drain well. Heat 2 tablespoons each oil and butter in a large, deep skillet over medium heat. Add the potatoes and cook for 5–6 minutes, turning once. Add 1 diced red bell pepper and fry for 2–3 minutes. Add 2¾ cups corn kernels to the skillet and stir in 1 chopped red chile, 6 sliced scallions, and 2 sliced garlic cloves. Season and cook for 5 minutes, until cooked through. Meanwhile, fry 4 eggs until cooked to your liking and serve the hash on warm plates topped with the eggs.

30 Corn and Red Pepper Frittata

Heat 2 tablespoons olive oil in medium, nonstick skillet over medium heat. Add 1 finely chopped red onion and cook for 2–3 minutes. Stir in 1½ cups frozen peas and cook for 1–2 minutes. Add 1 (11 oz) can corn kernels, drained, and 1 (13 oz) jar roasted red peppers, drained and coarsely chopped, and stir-fry for 1–2 minutes. Preheat the broiler to medium. Pour 4 lightly beaten eggs over the mixture, season well, and sprinkle with ¼ cup finely chopped parsley. Cook over low heat for 10 minutes or until the bottom of the frittata is set. Remove from the heat and place the skillet under the broiler for 3–4 minutes or until the top is set and lightly golden. Cut into thick wedges and serve warm or at room temperature, with a salad.

Smoked Cheese, Roasted Pepper, and Spinach Quesadillas

Serves 4

1 (12 oz) package baby spinach

1 (7 oz) jar roasted red peppers, drained and coarsely chopped

8 scallions, trimmed and finely chopped

8 oz smoked cheese, finely diced

1⅓ cups shredded mild cheddar cheese

1 red chile, seeded and finely chopped

¼ cup finely chopped cilantro

8 soft corn tortillas

salt and pepper

olive oil, for greasing

sour cream, to serve

- Blanch the spinach in a large saucepan of lightly salted boiling water for 1–2 minutes. Drain thoroughly through a fine strainer, pressing out all the liquid. Transfer to a bowl with the roasted pepper, scallions, smoked cheese, cheddar, chile, and cilantro. Season and mix well.

- Scatter one-quarter of the spinach mixture over a tortilla, top with another tortilla, and press together. Make 3 more quesadillas in the same way.

- Grease 2 large skillets with a little olive oil and place over medium heat. Put 1 quesadilla into each skillet and cook for 2 minutes, until golden. Invert onto a plate, then slide back into the skillet and cook for another 2 minutes, until the filling is hot and the cheese is just melting. Set aside while you cook the other 2.

- Cut each quesadilla into 4 and serve with sour cream.

---

1 **Roasted Pepper, Spinach, and Egg Noodle Stir-Fry** Heat 3 tablespoons light olive oil in a large wok or skillet and add 8 sliced scallions, 2 crushed garlic cloves, 1 sliced red chile, 1 (12 oz) jar roasted red peppers, drained and sliced, and 1 (12 oz) package baby spinach and stir-fry over high heat for 4–5 minutes or until the spinach has just wilted. Stir in 12 oz fresh egg noodles, cooked, and ⅓ cup sweet chili sauce, and cook for 1–2 minutes or until piping hot.

2 **Spicy Spinach, Roasted Pepper, and Smoked Cheese Burgers** Heat 2 tablespoons olive oil in a large wok or skillet and add 6 finely sliced scallions and 1 (6 oz) package baby spinach. Stir-fry for 5–6 minutes or until the spinach has wilted. Season and set aside. Split 4 burger buns, lightly toast, and spread 2 tablespoons of mayonnaise on each half. Drain 1 (7 oz) jar roasted peppers, slice, and divide among the bottom halves of the 4 burger buns, and top each with the spinach mixture and 2 slices of smoked cheese. Cover with the 4 toasted bun tops, press down lightly and serve.

VEG-SPEE-MOS

Herbed Bulgur and Chickpea Salad

Serves 4

1 (15 oz) can chickpeas, drained
½ cup cooked bulgur wheat
1 (7 oz) jar roasted red peppers,
  drained and chopped
large handful chopped dill
large handful chopped cilantro
⅓ cup olive oil
juice of 1 orange
1 teaspoon ground cumin
salt and pepper

· Place the chickpeas in a bowl with the bulgur wheat and roasted peppers. Add the dill and cilantro.

· Whisk together the olive oil, orange juice, and cumin and season well. Pour the dressing over the salad, toss to mix well, and serve immediately.

Herbed Middle Eastern Chickpea Pilaf Heat 2 tablespoons each butter and oil in a heavy saucepan. Add 1 chopped red onion, 2 chopped garlic cloves, 2 teaspoons ground cumin, and 1 teaspoon ground cinnamon and cook for 1–2 minutes. Add 2 cups instant long-grain rice, 1 (15 oz) can chickpeas, drained, ¼ cup finely chopped dill, and 4 cups hot vegetable stock. Season well, bring to a boil, cover, and reduce the heat to low. Cook for 10 minutes, then let stand for 8–10 minutes. Fluff up the grains with a fork and serve.

Turkish Chickpea and Bulgur Pilaf Heat 2 tablespoons olive oil in a large saucepan. Add 1 finely chopped red onion and cook over medium-low heat for 10–12 minutes, stirring often, or until the onion is lightly golden. Stir in 1 crushed garlic clove, 1 teaspoon ground cumin, 1 teaspoon ground cinnamon, and 1 cup bulgur wheat and cook, stirring, for 1–2 minutes, to lightly toast the grains. Pour over 1½ cups hot vegetable stock, stir well, then bring to a boil. Cover, reduce the heat to medium-low, and gently simmer for 6–8 minutes or until all the liquid is absorbed. Remove from the heat and add 1 (7 oz) jar roasted red peppers, drained and coarsely chopped, and 1 (15 oz) can chickpeas, without stirring them in. Cover and let stand for 5–10 minutes. Just before serving, remove the lid from the pilaf and fluff up the grains with a fork, mixing in the red peppers and chickpeas. Carefully fold in ½ cup finely chopped dill and ½ cup flat leaf parsley, along with 2 tablespoons finely chopped mint. Finally, scatter with goat cheese. Season to taste and serve hot, warm, or cold.

Cold Asian Summer Soba Noodle Salad

Serves 4

1 lb soba noodles, cooked
2 carrots, finely julienned
6 scallions, finely shredded
1 red bell pepper, finely sliced
¼ cup dark soy sauce
3 tablespoons sesame oil
1 tablespoon mirin
1 tablespoon superfine sugar
½ teaspoon chili oil

- Place the soba noodles in a wide bowl with the carrots, scallions, and bell pepper.

- In a separate bowl, mix together the soy sauce, sesame oil, mirin, sugar, and chili oil, then pour over the noodle mixture.

- Toss to mix well and serve chilled or at room temperature.

Warm Noodle and Edamame Salad

Bring a large saucepan of lightly salted water to a boil and add 8 oz soba noodles and 1⅔ cups frozen, shelled edamame (soybeans) and cook according to the package directions for the noodles. Drain and return to the saucepan with 6 sliced scallions. Cover and keep warm. Mix together 1 teaspoon grated fresh ginger root, 1 red chile, seeded and finely chopped, 1 tablespoon toasted sesame oil, 3 tablespoons mirin, 3 tablespoons light soy sauce, and 1 teaspoon honey. Pour over the noodle mixture and mix well. Sprinkle with 2 tablespoons toasted sesame seeds and ¼ cup finely chopped cilantro and serve.

Soba Noodle and Shiitake Mushroom Soup

Cook 8 oz soba noodles according to the package directions. Divide the noodles among 4 serving bowls. Meanwhile, place 4 cups hot vegetable stock, 3 tablespoons mirin, 8 oz sliced shiitake mushrooms, and ⅓ cup dark soy sauce in a saucepan and bring to a boil. Add 3 cups halved sugarsnap peas and continue to cook for 4–5 minutes, or until the sugarsnaps are cooked. Taste for seasoning, adding more soy sauce, if liked. Ladle the broth with some mushrooms and sugarsnaps over the soba noodles in the bowls and sprinkle with sliced scallions to serve.

VEG SPEE-RIU

Tortellini, Roasted Pepper, and Arugula Salad

Serves 4

2 (8 oz) store-bought fresh spinach and ricotta tortellini

1 (11 oz) roasted peppers in oil, drained

4 cups arugula

1 red onion, thinly sliced

1 cup fresh Italian-style salad dressing

black pepper

- Cook the tortellini according to the package directions.

- Meanwhile chop the roasted peppers and place in a bowl with the arugula and onion. Add the cooked tortellini.

- Pour over the salad dressing, toss to mix well, and serve sprinkled with black pepper.

Tortellini and Red Pepper Casserole Preheat the broiler to medium-high. Cook 2 (8 oz) packages store-bought fresh spinach and ricotta tortellini according to package directions, drain, and place in a lightly greased shallow ovenproof dish. Stir in 1 (12 oz) jar roasted red and yellow peppers in oil, drained and chopped, and 1 (14½ oz) can diced tomatoes with garlic and herbs, and toss to mix well. Season and pour over 1½ cups store-bought fresh cheese sauce to cover. Place under the broiler for 4–5 minutes or until the top is golden and bubbling. Serve warm with a arugula salad.

Red and Yellow Bell Pepper Tortellini Cut 1 red and 1 yellow bell pepper into large pieces, removing the seeds and membrane. Place skin side up under a hot broiler until the skin blackens and blisters. Cool in a plastic bag, then peel away the skin. Coarsely chopped the white sections of 8 scallions and place in a food processor with the roated peppers and 2 chopped cloves garlic, then process until chopped. Cook 2 (8 oz) packages store-bought fresh spinach and ricotta tortellini in a large saucepan of boiling water according to the package directions. Drain and return to the pan. Toss the roasted pepper mixture into the pasta and add ⅓ cup olive oil and ½ cup Parmesan cheese. Season to taste. Garnish with extra scallions and serve.

30 Creamy Mushroom and Herb Pancakes

Serves 4

2 tablespoons butter, plus extra for greasing

5 cups sliced cremini mushrooms

6 scallions, finely sliced

2 garlic cloves, crushed

2 cups store-bought fresh cheese sauce

1 (12 oz) package baby spinach

¼ cup finely chopped parsley

2 tablespoons finely chopped tarragon

8 store-bought pancakes

½ cup grated Parmesan cheese

salt and pepper

lettuce leaves, to serve

- Heat the butter in a large, nonstick skillet, add the mushrooms, scallions, and garlic, and sauté over high heat for 6–7 minutes.

- Stir in half of the cheese sauce and heat until just bubbling. Add the spinach and cook for 1 minute, until just wilted. Set aside, stir in the chopped herbs, and season.

- Take 1 pancake and spoon one-eighth of the filling down the center. Carefully roll the pancake up and put into a shallow, buttered gratin dish. Repeat with the remaining pancakes. Drizzle the remaining cheese sauce over the pancakes, sprinkle with grated Parmesan, and season to taste. Cook under a preheated medium-high broiler for 3–4 minutes, until piping hot and turning golden.

- Remove from the heat and serve with lettuce leaves.

---

10 Creamy Mushroom Spaghetti Cook 12 oz quick-cooking spaghetti according to the package directions. Meanwhile, process 10 oz cremini mushrooms in a blender with 2 cups store-bought fresh cheese sauce, then transfer to a large saucepan and bring to a boil. Simmer for 2–3 minutes, then stir in ¼ cup chopped tarragon. Drain the pasta and add to the mushroom mixture, mix well, season, and serve immediately.

20 Cheesy Garlic and Herb Stuffed Mushrooms Trim and remove the stems from 8 large, flat mushrooms and finely chop the stems. Heat 2 tablespoons butter in a nonstick skillet and add the chopped mushroom stems, 4 chopped scallions, and 1 crushed garlic clove. Sauté over high heat for 6–8 minutes. Season well and transfer to a bowl and mix with 1 cup cottage cheese, 1 tablespoon lemon zest, and 3 tablespoons each of chopped parsley and tarragon. Place the mushroom caps gill side up on a broiler rack in a single layer and season well. Divide the mushroom stem mixture among the caps, then sprinkle with ½ cup grated Parmesan. Position the broiler rack about 5 inches under a preheated medium-high broiler and cook for 6–8 minutes or until the tops are golden and bubbling. Line 4 serving plates with 2 cups spinach, top each plate with 2 stuffed mushrooms, and serve immediately.

QuickCook
Special Occasions

Recipes listed by cooking time

30

20

Jeweled Fruity Spicy Pilaf

Serves 4

1 tablespoon saffron threads

4 cups hot vegetable stock

2 cups basmati or long-grain rice

1 tablespoon olive oil

1 tablespoon butter

3 shallots, finely chopped

2 cloves garlic, finely chopped

4 cardamom pods, lightly bruised

2 cloves

2 cinnamon sticks

2 teaspoons cumin seeds

2 carrots, peeled and finely diced

¼ cup chopped dill

2 cups shelled edamame (soybeans)

⅔ cup golden rasins

¾ cup dried cranberries

seeds from 1 ripe pomegranate

⅓ cup slivered pistachio nuts

salt and pepper

- Add the saffron to the hot stock and set aside.

- Rinse the rice in cold running water and drain.

- Heat the oil and butter in a heavy saucepan over medium heat and sauté the shallots and garlic for 1–2 minutes.

- Add the cardamom pods, cloves, cinnamon sticks, cumin seeds, rice, and carrots and stir to mix well. Add the stock mixture along with the dill, season, and bring to a boil. Stir in the edamame, golden raisins, and dried cranberries. Cover tightly and reduce the heat to low. Cook for 10–12 minutes without lifting the lid.

- Remove from the heat and let stand, undisturbed, for 10 minutes.

- Remove the lid (the liquid should have been completely absorbed), stir in the pomegranate seeds and pistachio nuts, and serve immediately.

 Fruity Spiced Couscous

Place 2 cups couscous, cooked, in a wide bowl with 1 carrot cut into finely sticks, 2 finely sliced shallots, ⅔ cup golden raisins, 2 cups chopped dill, and ½ cup pomegranate seeds. Whisk together ⅓ cup olive oil with the juice of 1 orange and 1 teaspoon each of ground cinnamon and cumin. Pour the dressing over the couscous mixture. Season, toss to mix well, and serve.

Stir-Fried Fruity, Nutty Rice

Heat 2 tablespoons each butter and vegetable oil in a large wok or skillet. Add 1 thinly sliced onion and cook over medium-low heat for 10–12 minutes or until lightly golden. Stir in 4 cups cold, cooked basmati rice or long-grain rice with ½ cup vegetable stock and stir-fry over high heat for 4–5 minutes. Stir in ⅔ cup golden raisins, ¾ cup dried cranberries, ¾ cup pistachio nuts, and ¾ cup pine nuts, toasted. Stir-fry for 1–2 minutes or until piping hot and well mixed. Season and serve with plain yogurt.

30 Asparagus and Fontina Cheese Crespelles

Serves 4

1½ lb asparagus, woody ends trimmed

3 tablespoons olive oil

3 tablespoons freshly grated Parmesan cheese, plus extra to sprinkle

2 cups store-bought white sauce

freshly grated nutmeg, to taste

12 store-bought small pancakes

1 cup shredded fontina cheese, plus extra for sprinkling

- Place the asparagus in a roasting pan, toss with the oil, and roast in a preheated oven, at 475°F, for 7 minutes or until tender. Set aside.

- Reduce the oven temperature to 425°F.

- Stir the Parmesan into the white sauce and season with nutmeg. Spread a little sauce onto a pancake and top with one-twelfth of the asparagus and fontina. Roll up and place into a 2 quart ovenproof dish. Repeat with the remaining pancakes.

- Drizzle the remaining sauce over the pancakes in the dish, and sprinkle with the extra cheese and nutmeg. Bake for 12–15 minutes or until golden. Serve immediately.

---

1 Broiled Asparagus Bruschettas with Melted Fontina Blanch 1¼ lb asparagus tips in a saucepan of lightly salted boiling water for 2–3 minutes. Drain and divide the asparagus among 8 slices of toasted sourdough bread and scatter with 2 cups shredded fontina cheese. Broil under a preheated medium broiler for 2–3 minutes or until the cheese has just melted. Season and serve with a crisp green salad.

2 Herbed Asparagus and Fontina Souffléd Custards Lightly grease the insides of 4 ramekins with melted butter. Heat 2 tablespoons butter in a skillet and stir-fry 12 chopped asparagus spears and 6 chopped scallions for 3–4 minutes, then drain thoroughly in a metal strainer to remove the excess moisture and pat dry. Meanwhile, put 4 egg whites into a bowl and whisk until just stiff. In a separate bowl, beat 4 egg yolks and add the asparagus mixture, ⅓ cup each of chopped dill and chives, and 2 cups shredded fontina cheese. Stir in 1 tablespoon Dijon mustard, season, and, using a metal spoon, fold in the egg whites. Spoon the mixture into the ramekins, almost to the top. Bake in a preheated oven, at 425°F, for 12–15 minutes or until risen and lightly set. Serve immediately with a crisp lettuce and tomato salad.

Broccoli and Mushrooms in Black Bean Sauce with Noodles

Serves 4

1 tablespoon sunflower oil
¾ inch piece of fresh ginger root, sliced into matchsticks
3 cups small broccoli florets
8 oz shiitake mushrooms
6 scallions, sliced into ¾ inch pieces
1 red bell pepper, seeded and sliced
1¼ cups vegetable stock
1 lb fresh egg noodles
2 tablespoons light soy sauce
1 tablespoon cornstarch mixed to a paste with 2 tablespoons water

For the black bean sauce

1 tablespoon fermented salted black beans, rinsed well
1 tablespoon light soy sauce
2 garlic cloves, crushed
1 red chile, seeded and chopped
1 tablespoon Chinese rice wine

- Place all the ingredients for the black bean sauce in a food processor, blend until smooth, and set aside.

- Heat a wok over high heat and add the oil. When smoking, add the ginger and stir-fry for a few seconds. Add the broccoli and stir-fry for another 2–3 minutes.

- Add the mushrooms, scallions, and red bell pepper and stir-fry for 2–3 minutes.

- Add the black bean sauce and vegetable stock and bring to a simmer. Cook for 2–3 minutes, until tender.

- Meanwhile, cook the noodles according to the package directions, drain, and keep warm.

- Season with soy sauce to taste, mix in the blended cornstarch paste, and cook to thicken for 1 minute. Serve immediately with the egg noodles.

10 **Broccoli, Mushroom, and Black Bean Stir-Fry** Heat 1 tablespoon vegetable oil in a large wok and add 4 cups broccoli florets, 10 oz sliced shiitake mushrooms, and 6 sliced scallions. Stir-fry over high heat for 3–4 minutes, then add ½ cup store-bought black bean sauce and ½ cup water. Stir-fry over high heat for 3–4 minutes and serve over noodles.

30 **Asian Mushroom, Broccoli, and Black Bean Rice** Heat 2 tablespoons oil in a heavy saucepan and add 2 teaspoons each grated fresh ginger root and minced garlic, 8 sliced scallions, 10 oz sliced shiitake mushrooms, and 4 cups broccoli florets. Stir-fry for 3–4 minutes, then add 1⅔ cups long-grain rice. Stir to mix well and pour in 3 cups hot vegetable stock and ½ (15 oz) can black beans, rinsed and drained. Season, bring to a boil, cover tightly, and reduce the heat to low. Cook for 10–12 minutes, then remove from the heat (keeping the lid on) and let stand for another 10 minutes. Stir in ¼ cup light soy sauce, fluff up the grains of rice, and serve immediately.

Tagliatelle with Squash and Sage

Serves 4

7 cups peeled, seeded, and
  cubed butternut squash,
  acorn squash, or pumpkin
  (cut into ¾ inch cubes)
¼ cup olive oil
1 lb fresh tagliatelle
3 cups arugula
8 sage leaves, chopped
grated Parmesan cheese, to serve
  (optional)
salt and pepper

· Place the cubed squash into a small roasting pan, add
  2 tablespoons of the olive oil, season, and toss to mix well.
  Roast in a preheated oven, at 425°F, for 15–20 minutes or
  until just tender.

· Meanwhile, bring a large saucepan of salted water to a boil.
  Cook the pasta according to the package directions. Drain,
  return to the pan, then add the arugula, sage, and squash. Mix
  together over low heat with the remaining olive oil until the
  arugula has wilted, then serve with a good grating of fresh
  Parmesan cheese, if desired.

**Easy Pumpkin and
Sage Ravioli**
Cook 2 (8 oz) packages fresh
pumpkin-filled ravioli according
to the package directions.
Meanwhile heat ¼ cup butter
and ¼ cup olive oil in a large
skillet with 2 chopped garlic
cloves and 6 sage leaves over
medium-low heat. Drain the
ravioli and add to the skillet.
Season and toss gently to mix
well and serve, sprinkled with
1 cup grated Parmesan cheese.

 **Roasted Squash,
Tomato, and
Sage Soup** Place the roasted
squash from the above recipe
into a saucepan with 2½ cups
hot vegetable stock, 1 cup
tomato puree, and 1 tablespoon
finely chopped sage leaves.
Bring to a boil and simmer
for 12–15 minutes. Using an
immersion blender, process
the mixture until smooth. Stir
in ½ cup heavy cream and serve
with warm crusty bread.

30 Vegetable Pad Thai

Serves 4

10 oz flat rice noodles
3 tablespoons tamarind paste
3 tablespoons light soy sauce
3 tablespoons brown sugar
¼ cup vegetable oil
1 lb firm tofu, cut into ¼ inch strips, patted dry
3 garlic cloves, finely chopped
2 shallots, finely chopped
10 oz Asian mushrooms, torn or sliced
1–2 red chiles, seeded and finely chopped
2 extra-large eggs, beaten
bunch of scallions, sliced
1 carrot, halved and finely sliced
handful of fresh chives, snipped
bunch of fresh cilantro, chopped
⅔ cup chile roasted peanuts
2 limes, cut into wedges

- Place the noodles in a large bowl and cover with warm water. Let soak for 10–15 minutes or until soft, then drain.

- Meanwhile, make the sweet-and-sour paste. Mix the tamarind paste with a little hot water to loosen. Add the soy sauce and brown sugar, mix, taste, and adjust to produce a nice combination of sweet, salty, and sour.

- Heat 2 tablespoons of the oil in a wok or large skillet. Cook the tofu for 3–4 minutes, until golden and beginning to crisp. Remove from the wok, keep warm, and set aside.

- Heat the remaining oil in the wok and sauté the garlic and shallots for 30 seconds. Add the mushrooms and red chile and cook for 2 minutes, until beginning to soften. Add the noodles and stir-fry for 2 minutes, then push to one side.

- Add the eggs and let them set, then scramble and mix with the noodles. Add the sweet-and-sour paste and stir well. Toss in the onions, carrot, and tofu and cook for a few minutes.

- Divide among warm serving bowls, sprinkle with the herbs and peanuts, and serve with the lime wedges.

---

10 Thai Vegetable Salad

Cut 1 carrot, 8 scallions, and 1 cucumber into thin sticks and place in a large bowl with 2 thinly sliced Thai shallots and 10 oz firm tofu, diced. Make a dressing from the juice of 2 limes, ¼ cup Thai fish sauce, 3 tablespoons light soy sauce, ¼ cup sweet chili sauce, and 1 crushed garlic clove. Pour the dressing over the salad, season, and toss well. Garnish with ⅔ cup chopped roasted peanuts and serve.

20 Vietnamese-Style Vegetable Noodle Salad

Place 5 chopped garlic cloves in a bowl with 1 cup chopped cilantro and 1 finely chopped red chile. Add the juice of 1 lime, ¼ cup light soy sauce, 3 tablespoons Thai fish sauce, and 3 tablespoons sugar. Stir to mix and let the sauce stand for 5 minutes. Bring a large saucepan of salted water to a boil. Add 12 oz thin rice noodles and cook according to the package directions. Drain well and rinse the noodles with cold water to cool. Drain again. Combine the sauce mixture and noodles with 2 carrots cut into thin sticks, 1 shredded cucumber, and ¼ cup chopped mint in a large serving bowl. Toss well and serve the salad garnished with ⅔ cup chopped roasted peanuts.

Tarragon and Cheddar Cheese Soufflé Omelet

Serves 4

6 eggs
¼ cup chopped tarragon
1 cup shredded sharp cheddar cheese
2 tablespoons unsalted butter
crisp salad and crusty bread, to serve

- Separate the eggs and set aside the yolks. In a clean bowl, whisk the egg whites until stiff.

- Place the egg yolks in a separate bowl with the tarragon and cheddar cheese and lightly beat.

- Heat the butter in a large, heavy skillet. Carefully fold the egg white mixture into the egg yolk mixture and add to the skillet. Cook for 2–3 minutes over high heat, then place under a preheated medium-hot broiler for 3–4 minutes or until the top is souffléd and lightly golden.

- Serve immediately with a crisp salad and crusty bread.

Cheesy Tarragon and Pasta Gratin

Place 12 oz fusilli pasta, cooked, in a lightly greased, shallow ovenproof dish. Whisk together 4 eggs, ¼ cup finely chopped tarragon, ¼ teaspoon cayenne pepper, 2 teaspoons Dijon mustard, and 2 cups shredded cheddar cheese. Pour over the top of the pasta and toss to mix well. Sprinkle with 1 cup grated Parmesan cheese and bake in a preheated oven, at 425°F, for 15 minutes or until lightly golden on top. Serve immediately.

Cheese and Tarragon Soufflés

Brush four 1¼ cup ramekins with melted butter and sprinkle with 1 cup grated Parmesan cheese. Melt 4 tablespoons butter in a saucepan and add ⅓ cup all-purpose flour, ½ teaspoon English mustard powder, and a good pinch of cayenne pepper. Cook for a couple of minutes, then gradually add 1¼ cups milk, stirring continuously, until the mixture comes to a boil. Boil for 2 minutes, until thick. Remove from the heat, stir in 1 cup shredded sharp cheddar cheese, ¼ cup chopped tarragon, and 4 egg yolks, and season well. In a clean bowl, whisk 4 egg whites until stiff. Using a metal spoon, carefully fold the egg whites into the cheese mixture. Spoon the mixture into the ramekins, just up to the rim. Run your finger around the inside edge of the ramekins to help the soufflés rise straight up. Put on a preheated baking sheet in a preheated oven, at 425°F, and bake for 10–12 minutes or until risen and golden. Serve with a crisp salad.

20 Ravioli with Sweet Potato, Tomatoes, and Arugula

Serves 4

4 tablespoons butter

2 medium sweet potatoes, peeled and cut into ½ inch cubes

2 garlic cloves, chopped

small handful of fresh sage, chopped

grated zest of ½ lemon, plus a squeeze of juice

1⅓ cups halved cherry tomatoes

2 (8 oz) packages store-bought, fresh cheese-filled ravioli

salt and pepper

To serve

4 oz soft goat cheese, crumbled

large handful arugula

- Melt half the butter in a large skillet, add the chopped sweet potato, season well, then sauté over medium heat for about 5–6 minutes, until golden brown all over.

- Add the garlic, sage, and lemon zest and cook for 1 minute.

- Add the remaining butter, the cherry tomatoes, and lemon juice and gently sauté over low heat for 1 minute, until melted.

- Meanwhile, cook the ravioli according to the package directions. Drizzle with a little olive oil, then add the cooked pasta to the skillet with the sweet potato and cherry tomatoes, and carefully stir to coat with the sauce.

- Spoon into serving bowls and scatter with the goat cheese, arugula, and black pepper before serving.

---

10 Arugula, Tomato, and Ravioli Pasta

Salad Cook 2 (8 oz) packages store-bought, fresh cheese-filled ravioli according to the package directions, drain under cold water, and place in a wide salad bowl with a large handful of arugula, 4 oz goat cheese, crumbled, and 1⅓ cups halved cherry tomatoes. Whisk together ⅓ cup olive oil with 1 crushed garlic clove and the juice of 1 lemon. Season, pour over the top of the salad, and toss to mix well before serving.

30 Lemony Sweet Potato, Ravioli, and Cherry Tomato Casserole

Cook 2 (8 oz) packages store-bought, fresh cheese-filled ravioli according to the package directions, drain, and add to a lightly greased, medium baking dish along with 2 cups halved cherry tomatoes and 1 large finely diced, peeled sweet potato. In a bowl, whisk together 3 eggs with 1¼ cups heavy cream, 2 tablespoons lemon zest, 1 crushed garlic clove, 2 teaspoons finely chopped sage, and 4 oz goat cheese, crumbled. Pour over the ravioli mixture and bake in a preheated oven, at 400°F, for 20 minutes or until golden and bubbling. Serve immediately with an arugula salad.

Deep-Fried Haloumi Beer-Batter Fritters

Serves 4

2 cups all-purpose flour
1 egg, separated
1¼ cups ice-cold beer
½ cup ice-cold water
vegetable oil, for deep-frying
1 lb haloumi cheese or mozzarella
  cheese

To serve

arugula
lemon wedges

- Sift the flour into a large bowl and add the egg yolk. Gradually whisk in the lager, then add the measured water and whisk until well combined.

- Whisk the egg white in a separate bowl until stiff peaks form. Fold this into the batter.

- Fill a deep-fat fryer or a large, deep, heavy saucepan two-thirds full with vegetable oil. Heat the oil to 350°F or until a cube of bread turns golden in 10–15 seconds.

- Cut the haloumi into ½ inch slices, then dip into the batter to coat. Fry the haloumi in batches for 3–4 minutes, until crisp and golden-brown. Remove with a slotted spoon, season, and serve on a bed of arugula with wedges of lemon to squeeze over the top.

Bell Pepper and Haloumi Kebabs

Cut 2 red bell peppers, 2 yellow bell peppers, 2 red onions, and 10 oz haloumi cheese or mozzarella cheese into bite-size pieces and place in a bowl. Mix together 2 crushed garlic cloves, ½ cup olive oil, 2 teaspoons dried thyme, and the juice and grated zest of 1 lemon. Pour over the vegetables and cheese and toss to mix. Thread the vegetables and cheese alternately onto 12 metal skewers. Season and broil under a preheated medium-high broiler for 4–5 minutes on each side. Serve immediately.

Grilled Haloumi with Roasted

Peppers Cut 8 oz haloumi cheese or mozzarella cheese into slices 1 inch long and ¼ inch thick. Combine 1½ teaspoons ground sumac, 3 teaspoons finely grated lemon zest, and 3 tablespoons olive oil in a large bowl. Toss the haloumi gently in the oil mixture to coat, then season. Heat a heavy, ridged grill pan to medium-high. Slice 2 eggplants lengthwise and brush with olive oil. Cook the slices in batches for 2–3 minutes on each side or until lightly charred. Transfer to a wide bowl or platter. Cook the haloumi in the grill pan for 2–3 minutes on each side or until golden. Gently toss 1 (7 oz) jar roasted peppers in oil, drained and coarsely chopped, with the eggplant to combine. Divide among 4 serving plates and top with the haloumi. Whisk the juice of 1 large lemon with 3 tablespoons olive oil in a bowl, then season. Drizzle over the salad and serve garnished with 2 tablespoons each of chopped parsley and mint.

Malaysian Coconut and Vegetable Stew

Serves 4

2 tablespoons vegetable oil

1 medium onion, thinly sliced

⅓ cup laksa curry paste

2 (14 fl oz) cans coconut milk

1¼ cups water

1 teaspoon salt

2 medium potatoes, peeled and cut into ¾ inch pieces

4 carrots, peeled and cut into ¾ inch pieces

1 cup trimmed and halved green beans

1 cup cauliflower florets

2 cups peeled, seeded, and cubed butternut squash (cut into ¾ inch pieces)

½ cup cashew nuts

½ cup bean sprouts

4 scallions, trimmed and sliced on the diagonal

handful of Thai sweet basil or cilantro

- Heat the oil in a large saucepan over medium heat. Add the onion and the curry paste and sauté gently for 2–3 minutes, until it begins to smell fragrant.

- Add the coconut milk, measured water, and salt and bring to a boil.

- Add the potatoes and carrots and cook for 10 minutes, then add the green beans, cauliflower, and squash and cook for another 7 minutes.

- Add the cashew nuts and simmer for 3 minutes, until the vegetables are just tender.

- Stir in the bean sprouts, scallions, and basil or coriander. Simmer for 1 minute and serve immediately.

---

1 Quick Asian Coconut Soup

Heat 1 tablespoon vegetable oil in a large wok and add 6 chopped scallions, 1 tablespoon laksa curry paste, 1 (14 fl oz) can coconut milk, 1¾ cups vegetable stock, and 1 (10 oz) package stir-fry vegetables. Bring to a boil and cook over high heat for 4–5 minutes. Season and serve.

2 Spicy Coconut and Vegetable Noodles

Heat 1 tablespoon vegetable oil in a large wok or skillet and add 6 sliced scallions, 2 garlic cloves, 1⅔ cups finely shredded carrots, 2 cups finely shredded snow peas, and 1⅓ cups finely shredded red bell pepper. Stir-fry for 4–5 minutes. Meanwhile, prepare 12 oz dried stir-fry rice noodles according to the package directions and drain. Add 1 tablespoon laksa curry paste to the skillet and stir-fry for 1 minute, then add 1 cup coconut milk and stir-fry for 4–6 minutes. Add the drained noodles and heat through, season, and serve.

30 Nasi Goreng

Serves 4

2 extra-large eggs
3 tablespoons sunflower oil
1 tablespoon tomato paste
1 tablespoon ketjap manis
  (sweet dark soy sauce)
4 cups cold, cooked rice
1 tablespoon light soy sauce
2 inch piece cucumber, quartered
  lengthwise and sliced
salt and pepper
8 scallions, trimmed and thinly
  sliced on the diagonal, to garnish

For the spice paste

2 tablespoons vegetable oil
4 garlic cloves, coarsely chopped
⅓ cup coarsely chopped shallots
3 tablespoons roasted salted
  peanuts
6 medium-hot red chiles, seeded
  and coarsely chopped
1 teaspoon salt

- To make the spice paste, place all of the ingredients into a small food processor and process into a smooth paste, or grind using a mortar and pestle. Beat the eggs and season.

- Heat a little sunflower oil in a small skillet over medium-high heat, pour in one-third of the beaten egg, and cook until set on top. Flip, cook for a few additional seconds, then turn out and roll up tightly. Repeat twice with the remaining egg. Slice the omelets across into thin strips.

- Heat a wok over high heat until smoking. Add 2 tablespoons of the oil and the spice paste and stir-fry for 1–2 minutes.

- Add the tomato paste and ketchup manis and cook for a few seconds, then add the cooked rice and stir-fry over high heat for 2 minutes, until heated through.

- Add the strips of omelet and stir-fry for another minute before adding the soy sauce, cucumber, and most of the scallions and tossing together well.

- Spoon the nasi goring onto a large warm plate, scatter with the remaining scallions, and serve.

---

1 **Quick Spicy Rice Broth** Add 3 cups cold, cooked rice to a saucepan with 1 cup coconut milk, 2½ cups hot vegetable stock, 2 tablespoons tomato paste, and 1 tablespoon mild curry powder. Bring to a boil and cook over high heat for 4–5 minutes. Remove from the heat and stir in 6 finely shredded scallions and ¼ finely shredded cucumber. Season and serve in warm bowls.

2 **Indonesian Egg and Rice "Cake"** Heat 2 tablespoons oil in a large nonstick skillet. Beat 6 eggs in a large bowl with 3 tablespoons tomato paste, 1 tablespoon curry paste, 6 finely sliced scallions, 1 tablespoon ketjap manis, ⅓ cup finely chopped cilantro, and 1 finely chopped red chile. Add 3 cups cold, cooked rice and stir to mix well. Meanwhile, pour the mixture into the skillet and cook over medium heat for 8–10 minutes or until the bottom is lightly golden and set. Transfer to a preheated medium-high broiler for 3–4 minutes or until the top is set and golden. Serve immediately.

196 SPECIAL OCCASIONS

VEG-SPEC-MUV

Pesto and Antipasti Puff Tart

Serves 4

12 oz ready-to-bake puff pastry

3 tablespoons store-bought pesto

2 cups halved yellow and red cherry tomatoes

5 oz mixed antipasti (artichokes, roasted peppers, mushrooms, and eggplant), from a jar, drained

4 oz goat cheese, crumbled

basil leaves, to serve

- Lay the puff pastry on a baking sheet. Score a 1 inch margin around the edge and prick the bottom with a fork.

- Top with the pesto, cherry tomatoes, mixed antipasti, and goat cheese. Bake in a preheated oven, at 400°F, for 15–20 minutes.

- Top with the basil leaves and serve.

Spaghetti with Pesto and Cherry Tomatoes

Cook 12 oz quick-cooking spaghetti according to the package directions. Meanwhile, halve 3 cups cherry tomatoes and place in a wide bowl with a handful of basil. When the pasta is cooked, drain and add to the tomatoes with ½ cup fresh pesto, then garnish with ⅓ cup toasted pine nuts. Toss to mix well, season, and serve.

Antipasti and Pesto Pasta Salad

Cook 10 oz rigatoni or penne according to the package directions. Meanwhile, make the pesto by placing 1¼ cups basil, 3 tablespoons toasted pine nuts, ½ cup grated Parmesan cheese, 1 crushed garlic clove, and ½ cup olive oil in a blender and process until fairly smooth. Season with black pepper and place in a wide serving dish with 2 cups halved cherry tomatoes and 7 oz mixed antipasti (from a jar), then add the cooked pasta. Toss to mix well and serve at room temperature.

VEG-SPEC-DUO

 # Flash-in-the-Pan Ratatouille

Serves 4

½ cup olive oil

2 onions, chopped

1 eggplant, cut into ¾ inch cubes

2 large zucchini, cut into
  ¾ inch cubes

1 red bell pepper, seeded and cut
  into ¾ inch pieces

1 yellow bell pepper, seeded and
  cut into ¾ inch pieces

2 cloves garlic, crushed

1 (14½ oz) can diced tomatoes

2–3 tablespoons balsamic vinegar

1 teaspoon brown sugar

10–12 ripe black olives, pitted

salt and pepper

torn basil, to garnish

- Heat the oil in a large saucepan until hot and stir-fry all of the vegetables, except the tomatoes, for a few minutes.

- Add the tomatoes, balsamic vinegar, and sugar, season, and stir well. Cover tightly and simmer for 15 minutes, until the vegetables are cooked.

- Remove from the heat, scatter with the olives and torn basil, and serve.

 Mediterranean- Style Thick Vegetable Soup Blend the cooked ratatouille from the above recipe with 1¼ cups hot vegetable stock until smooth. Ladle into warm bowls and serve garnished with basil.

Grilled Vegetables Mediterranean Style Thinly slice 2 eggplants and 2 large zucchini lengthwise. Brush with olive oil and cook, in batches, on a smoking-hot, heavy, ridged grill pan for 2–3 minutes on each side. Transfer to a serving platter and add 1 (12 oz) jar roasted red peppers, drained and sliced, 2 finely chopped tomatoes, and 1 cup pitted ripe black olives. In a small bowl, whisk together ½ cup olive oil, 3 tablespoons balsamic vinegar, 1 teaspoon finely chopped rosemary, 1 crushed garlic clove, and 1 teaspoon brown sugar. Season and pour over the vegetables. Toss to mix well and serve garnished with basil.

Roasted Vegetable Couscous Salad

Serves 4

1 each red and yellow bell pepper, seeded and cut into 1 inch pieces

1 medium eggplant, cut into 1 inch pieces

1 zucchini, cut into 1 inch cubes

2 small red onions, peeled and cut into thick wedges

olive oil, to drizzle

1 cup couscous

6–8 preserved lemons, halved

a large handful of chopped mint and cilantro

⅓ cup pine nuts, toasted

5 oz feta cheese, crumbled

½ cup pomegranate seeds

salt and pepper

For the dressing

juice of 1 orange

⅓ cup olive oil

1 teaspoon ground cumin

½ teaspoon ground cinnamon

salt and pepper

- Place the vegetables on a large nonstick baking sheet. Drizzle with a little olive oil and season well. Roast in a preheated oven, at 400°F, for 15–20 minutes, or until the edges of the vegetables are just starting to char.

- Meanwhile, put the couscous in a wide bowl and pour over boiling hot water to just cover. Season well. Cover with plastic wrap and let stand, undisturbed, for 10 minutes or until all the liquid has been absorbed. Fluff up the grains with a fork and place on a wide, shallow serving platter.

- Make the dressing by mixing together the orange juice, olive oil, cumin, and cinnamon and season well.

- Fold the roasted vegetables, preserved lemons, and herbs into the couscous, pour over the dressing, and toss to mix well.

- Just before serving, scatter with the pine nuts, feta, and pomegranate seeds and serve immediately.

---

1 Lemon and Herb Couscous

Put 3 cups cooked couscous into a large bowl with ½ cup each chopped mint and cilantro, 6 sliced scallions, and 6 chopped preserved lemons. Season, toss to mix well, and serve, garnished with toasted pine nuts.

2 Roasted Vegetable Tabboulleh

Roast the vegetables as in the recipe above. While the vegetables are roasting, place 1⅓ cups bulgur wheat in a large bowl and pour over hot vegetable stock until just covered. Cover and let stand, undisturbed, for 15 minutes or until tender. Add 2 finely chopped garlic cloves, ⅓ cup olive oil, a large handful each of chopped flat leaf parsley and mint, and the roasted vegetables and their juices. Season, toss to mix well, and serve.

Spicy Szechuan Tofu and Vegetable Stir-Fry

Serves 4

¼ cup vegetable oil
6 scallions, finely sliced
2 red chiles, thinly sliced
1 inch piece of fresh ginger,
　finely chopped
4 garlic cloves, finely sliced
1 teaspoon crushed Szechuan
　peppercorns
pinch of salt
8 oz firm tofu, cut into
　1 inch cubes
3 cups halved snow peas
10 baby corn, halved lengthwise
3½ cups chopped bok choy
3 cups bean sprouts
2 tablespoons light soy sauce
2 tablespoons Chinese rice wine
sesame oil, for drizzling
cooked rice, to serve

· Heat 2 tablespoons of the oil in a wok or deep skillet and add the scallions, chiles, ginger, garlic, peppercorns, and a pinch of salt. Sauté for 1 minute, add the tofu, and stir-fry for another 2 minutes, then transfer to a plate.

· Heat the remaining oil and stir-fry the snow peas, corn, bok choy, and bean sprouts for a few minutes, until starting to wilt, then add the soy sauce and rice wine.

· Return the tofu mixture to the wok or skillet and toss everything together.

· Drizzle with sesame oil and serve with cooked rice.

Szechuan-Style Tofu Stir-Fry

Cube 1 lb firm tofu and broil under a preheated medium broiler for 2–3 minutes, until golden brown. Meanwhile, heat 2 tablespoons vegetable oil in a wok or deep skillet. Add 2 (10 oz) packages stir-fry vegetables and stir-fry for 3–4 minutes. Stir in ⅔ cup store-bought Szechuan stir-fry sauce and stir-fry for another 1–2 minutes. Add the tofu to the wok, toss to mix, and serve.

Noodle and Tofu Salad with Szechuan Peppercorns

In a large bowl, mix together ¼ cup light soy sauce, 3 tablespoons sweet chili sauce, grated zest and juice of 1 lemon, 2 chopped red chiles, 2 teaspoons Szechuan peppercorns, and 2 tablespoons water. Add 1 lb firm tofu, cubed, and let marinate for at least 25 minutes. Meanwhile, prepare 8 oz fine rice noodles according to the package directions. Drain and cool under running water.

Toss together the cooled noodles, 1 cup thinly sliced snow peas, 1 cup thinly sliced radishes, 1 thinly sliced red onion, and 1 tablespoon toasted sesame seeds. Gently stir in the tofu and marinade and divide among bowls. Scatter with cilantro and serve.

30 Autumnal Moroccan Vegetable Tagine

Serves 4

2 tablespoons olive oil
1 onion, halved and thickly sliced
3 garlic cloves, finely chopped
1 teaspoon finely grated fresh
  ginger root
1 teaspoon cinnamon
pinch of saffron threads
2 teaspoons ground cumin
4 teaspoons harissa paste
¼ cup tomato paste
3 tablespoons honey
1¾ lb mixed autumnal vegetables,
  such as squash, parsnips, and
  sweet potato, peeled and cubed
3 cups vegetable stock
salt and pepper
couscous, to serve
chopped cilantro, to garnish

- Heat the oil in a large nonstick saucepan and sauté the onion and garlic for 1–2 minutes.

- Add the ginger, cinnamon, saffron, ground cumin, harissa paste, tomato paste, honey, vegetables, and stock and bring to a boil.

- Season, cover, and simmer for 20 minutes or until the vegetables are tender.

- Serve with couscous and garnish with the chopped cilantro.

---

1 0 Moroccan-style Couscous Place 2 cups couscous in a bowl with 2 teaspoons harissa paste, 1 teaspoon each of ground cumin and cinnamon, a large pinch of saffron, ½ chopped onion, 3 tablespoons tomato paste, 1¼ cups chopped tomatoes, and 1 tablespoon honey. Pour in enough hot vegetable stock to just cover. Season, stir, cover, and let stand for 8 minutes or until all the liquid is absorbed. Fluff up with a fork, stir in ¼ cup chopped cilantro, and serve.

2 0 Moroccan-Style Root Vegetable Pasta Sauce Heat 2 tablespoons olive oil in a saucepan and add 1 chopped onion, 2 crushed garlic cloves, 1 teaspoon grated fresh ginger root, 1 teaspoon each of ground cumin and cinnamon, then stir-fry for 1–2 minutes. Add 1 (14½ oz) can diced tomatoes, 2 teaspoons harissa paste, and 1 cup hot vegetable stock. Stir in 1¼ lb mixed root vegetables (such as carrots, sweet potato, and parsnip), finely diced, and bring to a boil. Cook, uncovered, for 15 minutes or until the vegetables are tender. Season and serve over pasta.

Eggplant and Harissa Sauté

Serves 4

¼ cup sunflower oil
1½ lb baby eggplants, thinly
  sliced
4 tomatoes, chopped
1 teaspoon ground cinnamon
1 teaspoon finely chopped
  cilantro
2 tablespoons harissa
salt and pepper
cooked long-grain rice, to serve

· Heat the oil in a large skillet and add the eggplants.

· Sauté over high heat for 2–3 minutes, then add the tomatoes, cinnamon, cilantro, and harissa. Stir-fry for 3–4 minutes or until the eggplants are tender.

· Season to taste and serve with rice.

Crispy Moroccan-Style Eggplant and Harissa Fritters Cut 1½ lb eggplants into thin sticks and mix in a bowl with 2 tablespoons harissa paste, 1 teaspoon turmeric, 1 teaspoon crushed coriander, and some salt. Add 2¾ cups chickpea (besan) flour, a little at a time, stirring to coat the eggplant. Gradually drizzle cold water over the mixture, adding just enough to make a sticky batter. Fill a deep saucepan one-quarter full with sunflower oil and place over high heat until it reaches 350°F or a cube of bread it sizzles and turns golden in 10–15 seconds. Fry spoonfuls of the mixture in batches for 1–2 minutes or until golden brown and crisp on the outside. Remove with a slotted spoon and drain on paper towels. Serve with a minted yogurt dip.

Braised Baby Eggplants with Honey and Harissa Place 1 tablespoon finely grated fresh ginger root, 2 tablespoons finely grated garlic, and ½ (14½ oz) can diced tomatoes in a blender and process until smooth. Heat ½ cup sunflower oil in a large, heavy skillet over medium heat and cook 1¼ lb halved baby eggplants in batches, in a single layer, for 6–8 minutes or until lightly browned, turning once. Remove with a slotted spoon and drain on paper towels. Reheat the oil left in the skillet and add 1 teaspoon ground cumin, 2 teaspoons fennel seeds, and 2 teaspoons nigella seeds. Stir-fry for 1–2 minutes, then add the blended ginger, garlic, and tomato mixture. Stir-fry for 2–3 minutes, then add the remaining tomatoes from the can along with 1 teaspoon ground cinnamon, 1 teaspoon ground coriander, and 1 tablespoon rose harissa. Season well. Cook over medium heat, stirring often, for 10 minutes or until the mixture is smooth and thick. Stir in 1 tablespoon honey. Transfer the eggplants back to the skillet, toss gently to coat evenly, cover, and cook gently for 3–4 minutes. Remove from the heat and scatter with 2 tablespoons toasted pine nuts and ⅓ cup chopped cilantro. Serve with couscous or rice.

Broccoli and Blue Cheese Soufflés

Serves 4

4 tablespoons butter, plus extra melted butter for greasing
handful of fine fresh white bread crumbs
3½ cups broccoli florets
⅓ cup all-purpose flour
1¼ cups milk
1 teaspoon smoked paprika
grated fresh nutmeg
4 extra-large eggs, separated
4 oz creamy blue cheese, crumbled
salt and pepper

- Brush four 1¼ cup ramekins with melted butter and sprinkle with bread crumbs to coat the bottom and sides.

- Blanch the broccoli in boiling water until almost tender, then process in a blender until smooth.

- Melt the butter in a saucepan, add the flour, and cook for 2 minutes. Gradually add the milk, stirring continuously, and bring to a boil. Boil for 2 minutes, until thick.

- Remove from the heat and stir in the spices and egg yolks. Season well and stir in the pureed broccoli and the cheese.

- In a clean bowl, whisk the egg whites until stiff. Using a metal spooon, carefully fold the egg whites into the broccoli and cheese mixture.

- Pour into the ramekins, almost up to the rim. Run your finger around the inside edge of the ramekins to help the soufflés rise straight up. Bake on a preheated hot baking sheet in a preheated oven, at 400°F, for 8–10 minutes or until risen. Serve immediately.

---

1 **Thick Broccoli and Blue Cheese Soup**
Place 3 cups store-bought fresh vegetable soup in a saucepan with 4 cups finely chopped broccoli florets and bring to a boil. Simmer, uncovered, for 5–6 minutes, then blend with an immersion blender until smooth. Stir in 1 cup heavy cream and 4 oz creamy blue cheese, crumbled. Season and serve in warm bowls with crusty bread.

2 **Pasta with Griddled Broccoli and Blue Cheese** Cook 12 oz penne according to the package directions. Meanwhile, blanch 7 cups broccoli florets in a saucepan of boiling hot water for 3–4 minutes. Drain and toss with ¼ cup olive oil, then cook on a smoking-hot, heavy, ridged grill pan for 3–4 minutes or until just tender. Drain the pasta and return to the saucepan with the broccoli, 4 oz creamy blue cheese, crumbled, and 1 cup cream cheese. Season well. Sprinkle over ½ cup chopped toasted walnuts and serve with an arugula salad.

Scallion, Dill, and Chive Pancakes

Serves 4

1⅓ cups all-purpose flour
1 teaspoon baking powder
⅔ cup milk
2 extra-large eggs
4 tablespoons butter, melted
2 tablespoons each finely
   chopped dill and chives,
   plus extra to garnish
4 scallions, finely chopped
vegetable oil, for shallow-frying
salt and pepper

To serve

1 cup cream cheese, whisked with
   juice of 1 lemon
2 plum tomatoes, finely chopped

- Sift the flour and baking powder into a bowl with a pinch of salt. Beat the milk, eggs, butter, herbs, and scallions together in a separate bowl.

- Stir the wet mixture into the dry ingredients until the mixture comes together to form a smooth, thick batter.

- Heat a little vegetable oil in a small nonstick skillet and spoon in one-eighth of the batter. Cook the pancake for 1–2 minutes, or until bubbles form on the surface, then carefully turn it over and cook for another 1–2 minutes, or until golden brown on both sides. Remove the pancake and keep warm while the remaining pancakes are cooked; the batter makes 8 pancakes.

- Stack 2 pancakes on each serving plate and spoon over a dollop of the cream cheese mixture. Top with the chopped tomatoes and serve garnished with a sprinkling of herbs and freshly ground black pepper.

---

10 Scrambled Eggs with Dill, Chives, and Cream Cheese Beat together 6 eggs with 1 cup cream cheese, then add a small handful each of chopped chives and dill. Heat 2 tablespoons butter in a large skillet and add the egg mixture. Cook, stirring, until the eggs are scrambled. Season and serve over hot buttered toast.

30 Middle Eastern Scallion and Herb Soup Slice the white and green parts of 1½ lb scallions into 1 inch lengths and keep separate. Melt 4 tablespoons butter in a large saucepan, add ¼ cup olive oil, the white scallion slices, and 6 halved garlic cloves, then season. Sauté over medium heat for 4–5 minutes, until the vegetables are soft. Toss in the green scallion segments along with 3 bay leaves and cook for 10 minutes. Add 2 cups peas and 1 diced zucchini and cook for another 5 minutes. Remove half of the vegetables from the pan and set aside. Add 4 cups stock to the remaining vegetables, bring to a boil, and simmer for 3 minutes. Remove the bay leaves and add a small handful each of chopped dill and chives. Process until smooth with an immersion blender before returning the reserved vegetables to the pan and warming gently. Stir in 1 cup cream cheese until combined. Transfer the soup into individual bowls and serve.

Grilled Asparagus with Caper Dressing and Duck Eggs

Serves 4

1 tablespoon olive oil, plus extra
  for drizzling
1¼ lb asparagus spears
4 duck eggs
4 slices sourdough bread, toasted
2 tablespoons olive oil
2 medium tomatoes
salt and pepper

For the dressing

2 tablespoons capers, rinsed
  and drained
⅓ cup olive oil
2 tablespoons red wine vinegar
1 teaspoon Dijon mustard
1 garlic clove, crushed
2 teaspoons crushed pink
  peppercorns

- Blanch the asparagus spears for 1–2 minutes.

- Place the tomatoes on a baking sheet lined with nonstick parchment paper, drizzle with a little olive oil, season, and roast in a preheated oven, at 400°F, for 10–12 minutes.

- Meanwhile, toss the asparagus with the olive oil and heat a heavy, ridged grill pan until smoking. Cook the asparagus for 4 minutes, turning once. Remove and divide among 4 plates.

- Fry the eggs in a skillet or until cooked to your liking. Add a slice of toasted sourdough to each plate and top with the fried egg.

- Mix together all the ingredients for the dressing, season, and drizzle the dressing over the asparagus and eggs.

- Serve immediately with the roasted tomatoes.

10 Asparagus, Lettuce, and Duck Egg Salad Blanch 1¼ lb asparagus tips in a saucepan of lightly salted boiling water for 3 minutes. Drain and place on a platter with 2 halved or quartered medium tomatoes, 2 shelled and quartered, hard-boiled duck eggs, and the leaves from 2 Boston lettuce. Make the dressing: whisk together ⅓ cup olive oil, 2 tablespoons red wine vinegar, 1 teaspoon Dijon mustard, and 1 crushed garlic clove, then season well. Pour over the salad and toss to mix before serving.

20 Spanish-Style Asparagus and Tomato Tortilla Cut 1¼ lb asparagus tips in half. Using a fork, gently beat 6 eggs in a bowl with 1 cup grated Parmesan cheese and 2 tablespoons chopped basil, then season well. Heat ¼ cup olive oil in an ovenproof skillet over high heat and add 2 chopped garlic cloves, 6 chopped medium tomatoes, and the asparagus. Toss together and cook for 2 minutes or until the garlic starts to change color. Add the egg mixture to the skillet, distributing it evenly without stirring. Once the eggs start to set around the sides, place under a preheated medium-high broiler for 3–4 minutes, or until set and golden and fluffy. Serve with a mixed salad.

 # Lemon and Herb Risotto

Serves 4

1 tablespoon olive oil
3 shallots, finely chopped
2 cloves garlic, finely chopped
½ head celery, finely chopped
1 zucchini, finely diced
1 carrot, peeled and finely diced
1½ cups risotto rice
5 cups hot vegetable stock
good handful fresh mixed herbs
　(tarragon, parsley, chives, dill)
¼ lb (1 stick) butter
1 tablespoon finely grated
　lemon zest
1 cup freshly grated Parmesan
　cheese
salt and pepper

- Heat the oil in a heavy saucepan and add the shallots, garlic, celery, zucchini, and carrot and sauté slowly for 4 minutes or until the vegetables have softened. Add the rice and turn up the heat. Stir-fry for 2–3 minutes.

- Add a ladleful of hot stock followed by half the herbs and season well.

- Reduce the heat to medium-low and add the remaining stock, 1 ladleful at at time, stirring continuously, until each amount is absorbed and the rice is just firm to the bite but cooked through.

- Remove from the heat and gently stir in the remaining herbs, butter, lemon zest, and Parmesan. Place the lid on the pan and let sit for 2 to 3 minutes, during which time it will become creamy and oozy. Serve immediately, sprinkled with freshly ground black pepper.

1 Lemon and Vegetable Rice

Heat 1 tablespoon olive oil in a large skillet and add 2 chopped shallots, 2 chopped garlic cloves, and 1 (10 oz) package stir-fry vegetables. Add 4 cups cold, cooked rice and the zest and juice of 1 small lemon. Stir-fry for 5–6 minutes or until piping hot. Serve immediately.

2 Lemon and Herb Tagliatelle

Heat 1 tablespoon oil in a large skillet and add 2 chopped shallots, 1 chopped garlic clove, ½ finely diced carrot, and 1 finely diced celery stick. Sauté over medium heat for 4–5 minutes. Meanwhile cook 12 oz tagliatelle according to the package directions. Drain and add to the skillet with a large handful of chopped mixed herbs, along with the juice and finely grated zest of 1 small lemon. Sprinkle with 1 cup grated Parmesan cheese and serve.

10 Asparagus and Udon Noodle Stir-Fry

Serves 4

2 tablespoons sunflower oil
2 garlic cloves, crushed
12 oz asparagus tips
8 scallions, sliced diagonally
12 oz straight-to-wok udon noodles
⅓ cup oyster sauce
⅓ cup water

- Heat the oil in a large skillet. Add the garlic and asparagus tips and stir-fry for 2 minutes.

- Add the scallions, noodles, oyster sauce, and water and toss together. Stir-fry for another 2 minutes, then serve immediately.

---

20 Asparagus, Beans, and Udon Noodle Bowl

Combine 3 tablespoons dark soy sauce, 2 tablespoons rice vinegar, 1 tablespoon mirin, and 2 tablespoons sugar in a shallow bowl and stir until the sugar has dissolved. Add 10 oz firm tofu, cut into bite-size cubes, and turn to coat. Let absorb the flavors for at least 15 minutes. When ready to cook, turn the oven on to low and heat an ovenproof plate. Scatter 2 tablespoons cornstarch over a separate plate. Remove the tofu from the marinade, reserving the marinade, and roll the tofu in the cornstarch to coat. Heat a wide skillet over medium-high heat and add enough sunflower oil to cover the bottom. Fry the tofu, using tongs to turn, until dark golden and crisp all over. Drain on paper towels, then keep warm by placing on the plate in the oven. Meanwhile, pour 4 cups vegetable stock into a medium saucepan with the reserved marinade and bring to a boil. Add 12 oz asparagus tips, ⅓ cup shelled edamame (soybeans), ⅓ cup frozen peas, 1 teaspoon grated fresh ginger root, and 12 oz straight-to-the-wok udon noodles and simmer for 3–4 minutes, until the vegetables are just tender. Divide among 4 bowls, then divide the tofu cubes among each. Top with ½ cup coarsely chopped cilantro and serve drizzled with a little chili oil.

30 Udon Noodle Pancakes with Grilled Asparagus

Cook 7 oz udon noodles according to the package directions. Drain and set aside. Heat 2 tablespoons vegetable oil in a skillet over high heat. Divide the noodles into 12 portions and cook in batches. Flatten with a spatula, so the surface browns, reduce the heat to medium-high, and cook the noodle "pancakes" for 3–4 minutes or until golden and crispy on the bottom. Turn and cook for 1–2 minutes, again flattening as they cook. Remove and keep warm. Heat a heavy, ridged grill pan until smoking. Brush 12 oz asparagus tips with oil and sear for 2–3 minutes on each side. Transfer to a bowl and mix with ⅓ cup oyster sauce and 3 tablespoons sweet chili sauce. Serve the noodle "pancakes" immediately topped with the asparagus mixture.

30 Tomato, Camembert, Goat Cheese, and Herb Tart

Serves 4

8 oz ready-to-bake puff pastry

3–4 tablespoons black olive tapenade or Dijon mustard, if preferred

5 ripe plum tomatoes, finely sliced

8 large basil leaves, roughly torn

4 oz Camembert cheese

4 oz goat cheese

2 tablespoons fresh thyme, plus extra to garnish

1–2 tablespoons extra virgin olive oil

salt and pepper

- Roll out the pastry and use it to line a 10 inch tart pan.

- Spread the tapenade or mustard over the bottom of the tart.

- Discarding any juice or seeds that have run from the tomatoes, lay the slices in concentric circles in the tart. Season the tomatoes (keep in mind that tapenade is salty) and scatter with the basil.

- Cut the Camembert into thin wedges and the goat cheese into thin wedges or slices, according to its shape. Arrange a circle of Camembert pieces around the outside and a circle of goat cheese within. Put any remaining pieces of cheese in the middle.

- Sprinkle with the thyme leaves and drizzle the oil on top.

- Bake in a preheated oven, at 400°F, for 15–18 minutes, until the pastry is cooked and the cheese is golden and bubbling. Serve immediately, garnished with thyme.

10 Tomato, Tapenade, and Two Cheese

Baguette Split 2 warm baguettes and spread both sides with ⅔ cup black olive tapenade and ⅓ cup Dijon mustard. Fill each with 6 ripe, sliced plum tomatoes, 1 cup basil, 4 oz each of Camembert cheese and goat cheese, sliced. Season and serve with a green salad.

20 Fresh Tomato and Two Cheese Pasta

Cook 12 oz farfalle pasta according to the package directions. Meanwhile, finely chop 4 plum tomatoes, 1 cup pitted ripe black olives, 1 cup basil, and 2 tablespoons thyme, and place in a bowl with 4 oz each of goat cheese and Camembert cheese, diced. Drain the pasta and add to the tomato mixture. Season, toss to mix well, and serve immediately.

Lima Bean and Vegetable Nut Casserole

Serves 4

6 tablespoons butter, chilled and diced

1⅓ cups all-purpose flour

1 cup chopped walnuts

½ cup shredded cheddar cheese

2 (8 oz) packages prepared broccoli, cauliflower, and carrots

2 cups store-bought tomato and herb sauce

2 garlic cloves, crushed

⅓ cup finely chopped basil

1 (15 oz) can lima beans, drained and rinsed

salt and pepper

- Rub the butter into the all-purpose flour until crumbs form. Stir in the chopped walnuts and shredded cheese, season, and set aside.

- Remove the carrots from the packages of prepared vegetables, coarsely chop, and boil for 2 minutes. Add the broccoli and cauliflower and cook for 1 minute, then drain.

- Meanwhile, heat the tomato and herb sauce in a large saucepan until bubbling.

- Stir in the garlic, basil, lima beans, and blanched vegetables. Transfer to a medium ovenproof dish and scatter the crumble mixture over the top. Bake in a preheated oven, at 400°F, for 15–20 minutes or until golden and bubbling.

1 Lima Bean and Walnut Pâté

Add 2 (15 oz) cans lima beans, drained, and the juice and finely grated zest of 1 lemon to a food processor with 1 crushed garlic clove, ¼ cup each of finely chopped basil and mint, ½ cup chopped walnuts, ½ cup mayonnaise, and 2 teaspoons Dijon mustard. Blend until smooth and serve spread thickly on toasted sourdough bread with a salad.

2 Vegetable and Lima Bean Soup

Lightly sauté 2 sliced garlic cloves and 1 chopped onion in 2 tablespoons olive oil for 1–2 minutes. Add 4 cups hot vegetable stock, 2 (8 oz) packages prepared broccoli, cauliflower, and carrots, ¼ cup chopped parsley, and 2 (15 oz) cans lima beans, drained, to the onion, and simmer for 15 minutes. Let the soup cool slightly, then blend two-thirds using an immersion blender. Return the blended soup to the vegetables along with 2 tablespoons tomato paste and mix well. Serve immediately, garnished with a little chopped parsley, if desired.

Quick Curried Egg Salad

Serves 4

8 hard-boiled eggs
4 tomatoes, cut into wedges
2 Boston lettuce, leaves
  separated
¼ cucumber, sliced
1 cup plain yogurt
1 tablespoon mild curry powder
3 tablespoons tomato paste
juice of 2 limes
⅓ cup mayonnaise
thyme, to garnish
salt and pepper

- Halve the eggs and place on a large platter with the tomatoes, lettuce leaves, and cucumber.

- Mix the yogurt together with the curry powder, tomato paste, lime juice, and mayonnaise. Season the dressing, then pour it over the salad. Serve immediately, garnished with thyme.

2 Indian-Style Spicy Open Omelet

Heat 2 tablespoons of vegetable oil in a large ovenproof skillet. Add 1 chopped onion, 1 chopped red chile, 2 teaspoons cumin seeds, 1 teaspoon each of grated fresh ginger root and garlic, 1 teaspoon curry powder, and 1 finely chopped tomato. Stir-fry for 3–4 minutes. Beat together 6 eggs and a small handful of finely chopped cilantro. Season and pour over the vegetable mixture in the skillet. Cook over low heat for 8–10 minutes or until the bottom is starting to set, then place under a preheated hot broiler for 3–4 minutes or until the top is set and lightly colored. Remove and serve with warm naan and a salad.

3 Egg and Tomato Curry Heat

2 tablespoons sunflower oil in a large, nonstick wok or skillet. Add 1 tablespoon cumin seeds, 1 tablespoon black mustard seeds, 2 crushed garlic cloves, 2 dried red chiles, and 10 fresh curry leaves, then stir-fry for 30–40 seconds. Add 1 halved and thinly sliced onion and 2 tablespoons curry powder, then stir in ¾ cup canned diced tomatoes, 1 teaspoon sugar, and 1 cup coconut milk. Bring to a boil, reduce the heat to medium-low, and cook for 8–10 minutes, stirring often. Add 8 shelled, hard-boiled eggs and cook for 10–12 minutes, until the sauce is thickened. Season with salt, garnish with cilantro, and serve with warm naan.

QuickCook
Dessert in a Dash

Recipes listed by cooking time

30

20

10

Quick Mini Lemon Meringue Pies

Serves 4

4 individual pastry crusts

¾ cup prepared lemon-flavored pudding and pie filling or lemon curd

1 egg white

¼ cup superfine sugar

- Fill each pastry crust with 3 tablespoons of the lemon curd or pie filling.

- In a large, clean bowl, whisk the egg white until it forms soft peaks and hold its shape. Gradually whisk in the sugar, a little at a time, until the mixture is thick and glossy.

- Pipe the meringue mixture in swirls over the lemon curd and bake on the top shelf of a preheated oven, at 400°F, for 5–6 minutes or until the meringue is just beginning to brown. Cool slightly and serve.

Lemon Meringue and Blueberry

Desserts Coarsely crush 2 meringue nests and place in 4 individual dessert bowls. Whip 1 cup heavy cream until if forms soft peaks, then stir in ½ cup prepared lemon-flavored pudding and pie filling or lemon curd to create a marbled effect. Spoon this mixture over the crushed meringue and top each with 3 tablespoons blueberries.

Luxurious Lemon Tart

Sift 1 cup all-purpose flour into a mixing bowl. Add 4 tablespoons cool, diced butter and rub in until the mixture resembles bread crumbs. Stir in 3 tablespoons confectioners' sugar. Lightly beat 1 egg yolk with 1 tablespoon cold water, add to the flour mixture, and mix with a rubber spatular. Gather together to form a soft dough. Roll out the dough and use to line a 9 inch tart pan. Line with parchment paper and fill with pie weights or dried beans. Bake in a preheated oven, at 350°F, for 12–15 minutes, then remove the paper and weights and bake for 5–8 minutes or until lightly golden. Let cool. Spoon in 2 cups prepared lemon-flavored pudding and pie filling or lemon curd. Whisk 1 cup heavy cream and spread over the lemon curd. Cut into wedges and serve.

Baked Amaretto Figs

Serves 4

8–12 ripe figs (depending on their size; 2 or 3 per person)

4 large oranges, peeled and cut into thick slices

¾ cup amaretto liqueur

⅔ cup sweet white wine

¼ cup superfine sugar

⅔ cup mascarpone cheese, lightly beaten

¼ cup finely chopped pistachio nuts

- Trim the end of the stems from each fig and cut in half.

- Place the orange slices in a shallow ovenproof dish and top with the fig halves.

- Mix together the amaretto, wine, and sugar and pour over the fruit mixture. Cover loosely with aluminum foil and bake in a preheated oven, at 400°F), for 10–12 minutes.

- Divide the mixture among 4 warm plates and spoon over the syrup from the dish.

- Serve with a big dollop of mascarpone cheese and the pistachios sprinkled over the top.

---

1 ### Fig, Orange, Amaretto, and

Blue Cheese Salad Thinly slice 12 ripe figs and place on a platter with 2 segmented oranges. Scatter with 4 oz creamy blue cheese, diced. Make a dressing by whisking together the juice of 1 orange and ¼ cup amaretto, and pour the dressing over the salad. Scatter ½ cup chopped pistachio nuts over the top and serve.

2 ### Broiled Fig and Amaretto Desserts

Thickly slice 12 figs and place on a lightly oiled broiler rack. Sprinkle with ¼ cup superfine sugar and put under a preheated hot broiler for 4–5 minutes. Whisk together 1 cup heavy cream until it forms soft peaks, then stir in ¼ cup amaretto. Divide the figs among 4 individual dessert bowls and top with the amaretto cream. Sprinkle 1 cup chopped pistachio nuts over the top and serve immediately.

Berry, Honey, and Yogurt Desserts

Serves 4

3½ cups frozen mixed berries, thawed

juice of 1 orange

⅓ cup honey

2 cups vanilla yogurt

½ cup granola

- Process half the berries with the orange juice and honey in a blender until smooth.

- Transfer to a bowl and stir in the remaining berries.

- Divide one-third of the berry mixture among 4 individual dessert glasses or small bowls. Top with half the yogurt.

- Layer with half the remaining berry mixture and top with the remaining yogurt.

- Top with the remaining berry mixture and sprinkle over the granola just before serving.

2 Berry and Orange Yogurt Smoothie

Peel and segment 2 large oranges and place the segments in a blender. Add 3 cups vanilla yogurt and 3½ cups frozen mixed berries. Spoon in ¼ cup honey and blend until thick and smooth. Pour into 4 chilled glasses and serve immediately.

3 Berry and Yogurt Phyllo Tarts

Cut 2 large sheets of phyllo pastry in half and cut each half into 4 squares. Brush each square with melted butter. Stack 4 squares on top of each other, then repeat with the remaining squares to create 4 stacks. Use to line four 4 inch tart pans. Bake the phyllo shells for 8–10 minutes in a preheated oven, at 350°F, until crispy and golden. Let cool and remove from the pans. To serve, place 2 tablespoons vanilla yogurt into each phyllo shell and spoon over 1¾ cups mixed berries. Dust with confectioners' sugar and serve immediately.

VEG-DESS-QIH

30 Blackberry Crisp

Serves 4

5 cups (about 1½ lb) blackberries
2 oranges, segmented
zest and juice of 1 orange
½ lb (2 sticks) butter
1¾ cups all-purpose flour
½ cup firmly packed brown sugar
cream or ice cream, to serve
(optional)

- Mix the blackberries, orange segments, and orange zest and juice together in a bowl.

- In a separate bowl, rub together the butter and flour with your fingertips until the mixture resembles bread crumbs, then stir in the sugar.

- Transfer the blackberry mixture to a large pie plate and scatter the crumb mixture over the top to cover.

- Bake in a preheated oven, at 425°F, for 20–25 minutes, until golden. Remove from the oven and serve warm with cream or ice cream, if liked.

---

1 **Blackberry, Orange, and Vanilla Puddings** Divide 1¼ cups prepared instant vanilla pudding or freshly prepared custard among 4 dessert glasses. Process 1⅓ cups blackberries in a blender with ¼ cup superfine sugar until smooth and spoon over the pudding in the glasses. Peel and segment 2 large oranges and layer on top of the blackberry puree. Top each glass with a small scoop of vanilla ice cream and serve.

2 **Spiced Blackberry Chutney** In a large saucepan, stir together 4 cups blackberries, ¾ cup superfine sugar, 1 sliced small red onion, 1 tablespoon grated ginger, and 1 tablespoon Dijon mustard. Cook over medium heat, stirring continuously, until the blackberries burst. Season to taste. Add ½ cup white wine vinegar and simmer, uncovered, for 10 minutes. Let the mixture cool slightly, then transfer to a warm sterilized jar and seal immediately.

Cherry and Vanilla Brûlée

Serves 4

2 cups pitted and coarsely chopped cherries
¾ cup superfine sugar
¼ cup coarsely chopped candied cherries
¼ cup kirsch or cherry liqueur
1¾ cups vanilla yogurt

· Mix the fresh cherries in a bowl with the half the sugar, the chopped candied cherries, and kirsch.

· Spoon the cherry mixture into 4 individual glass ramekins and top with the yogurt.

· Sprinkle the remaining superfine sugar over the yogurt and use a blowtorch (or place the ramekins under a preheated hot broiler for 2–3 minutes) to caramelize the tops. Serve immediately.

---

10 Cherry and Raspberry Brûlée

Place a mixture of 2 cups pitted cherries and 2½ cups raspberries in a shallow, ovenproof dish. Spoon 1¾ cups prepared vanilla pudding or custard on top and sprinkle with ¼ cup superfine sugar. Cook under a preheated medium-high broiler for 4–5 minutes or until lightly browned and bubbling. Serve immediately.

30 White Chocolate, Vanilla, and Cherry Cookies Beat ½ lb (2 sticks) unsalted butter, ⅓ cup firmly packed brown sugar, ⅓ cup granulated sugar, 1–2 drops of vanilla extract, and 1 egg until smooth. In a separate bowl, mix 2 cups all-purpose flour with 3 teaspoons baking powder and ½ teaspoon salt, then mix into the butter and sugar mixture with ½ cup white chocolate chips and ⅓ cup chopped candied cherries. Spoon about 20 mounds onto nonstick baking sheets. Give each mound plenty of space because the cookies spread as they bake. Bake in a preheated oven, at 375°F, for 12–14 minutes, until just golden, but still pale and soft in the middle. Let cool on the baking sheets for 5 minutes before lifting onto wire racks, then let cool completely.

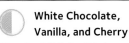

Molten Chocolate Lava Cakes

Serves 4

¼ lb plus 2 tablespoons (1¼ sticks)
  butter, cubed, plus extra
  for greasing
¼ cup unsweetened cocoa
  powder
8 oz semisweet dark chocolate
  (at least 70 percent cocoa
  solids), broken into pieces
2 eggs, plus 2 egg yolks
⅔ cup superfine sugar
3 tablespoons all-purpose flour
crème fraîche or whipped cream,
  to serve

- Grease four 1 cup molds or ramekins and dust with half the cocoa powder. Place on a baking sheet.

- Put the chocolate and butter in a heatproof bowl over a saucepan of just-simmering water. Stir occasionally until melted, smooth, and glossy. Set aside to cool.

- Meanwhile, beat the eggs, egg yolks, and sugar in a bowl for 5 minutes, until thick and foamy.

- Whisk the cooled chocolate mixture into the egg mixture, then sift in the flour and remaining cocoa and fold in.

- Divide the mixture among the molds or ramekins. Bake the cakes in a preheated oven, at 350°F, for 14–16 minutes or until the outsides are set but the insides are still soft. Hold each mold with a cloth, then carefully run a sharp knife around each cake and invert onto a warm plate. Alternatively, serve in the ramekins if using. Accompany with a scoop of cold crème fraîche.

Chocolate and Banana Pancakes

Melt 8 oz semisweet dark chocolate in a small saucepan. Place 4 small store-bought pancakes onto 4 serving plates and slice a banana into the center of each one. Drizzle over the melted chocolate and serve.

Chocolate and Honeycomb

Toffee Mousses Break 4 oz milk chocolate into pieces and melt gently in a small saucepan, then stir in 2 (1½ oz) chocolate-coated honeycomb toffee (sponge candy) bars, coarsely broken up. Gently stir 1¼ cups heavy cream into 8 oz mascarpone until combined, then stir in the chocolate mixture to create a marbled effect. Spoon into small glasses or cups, dust with unsweetened cocoa powder, and serve.

Spiced Pancakes with Ice Cream and Chocolate Sauce

Serves 4

2 cups all-purpose flour
3 teaspoons baking powder
1 teaspoon ground cinnamon
1 teaspoon allspice
¼ cup superfine sugar
1 egg
1¼ cups milk
sunflower oil, for shallow-frying

To serve

4 scoops vanilla ice cream
½ cup store-bought
   chocolate sauce

- Place the flour, baking powder, cinnamon, allspice, and sugar in bowl and make a well in the center.

- Beat the egg and pour into the center of the flour mixture.

- Gradually add the milk, beating well until smooth.

- Heat a little oil in a heavy skillet or flat griddle pan until moderately hot.

- Working in batches, drop large tablespoons of the batter into the skillet and cook for 1–2 minutes, until bubbles appear on the surface and the underneath is golden brown. Turn the pancake over and cook the other side for 1–2 minutes. Place a dish towel or paper towel between each pancake and keep warm on a preheated plate in a preheated oven, at 300°F. Repeat until all the batter has been used.

- Serve 3 pancakes per person with scoops of vanilla ice cream and drizzle the chocolate sauce over the top.

---

1 Cinnamon and Allspice Cookies

Cream ¼ lb (1 stick) softened butter with ⅓ cup firmly packed brown sugar, 1 teaspoon ground cinnamon, and ¼ teaspoon allspice, then beat in 1 egg and 1⅓ cups all-purpose flour sifted with 2 teaspoons baking powder. Drop spoonfuls of the mixture onto a baking sheet lined with parchment paper and bake in a preheated oven, at 350°F, for 8–10 minutes. Remove and let cool on racks.

2 Ricotta Pancakes with Chocolate

Sauce Sift together ⅔ cup all-purpose flour, 1 teaspoon baking powder, 1 teaspoon ground cinnamon, ½ teaspoon salt, and 2 tablespoons superfine sugar into a large bowl. Whisk 2 egg yolks, ⅓ cup buttermilk, and 3 tablespoons melted butter and gently mix into the dry ingredients. Carefully fold in 4 oz ricotta. Whisk the 2 egg whites until they form soft peaks, then gently fold them into the batter one-third at a time. Heat a little butter in a large ovenproof skillet, then add about 3 tablespoons of batter for each pancake, spaced apart. Put the skillet into a preheated oven, at 325°F, for 4 minutes, then remove and flip the pancakes. Return to the oven for another 4 minutes or until the pancakes feel firm to the touch. Place a pancake on each plate, drizzle some store-bought chocolate sauce over them, and serve with a dollop of crème fraîche or whipped cream on the side.

VEG-DESS-BIU

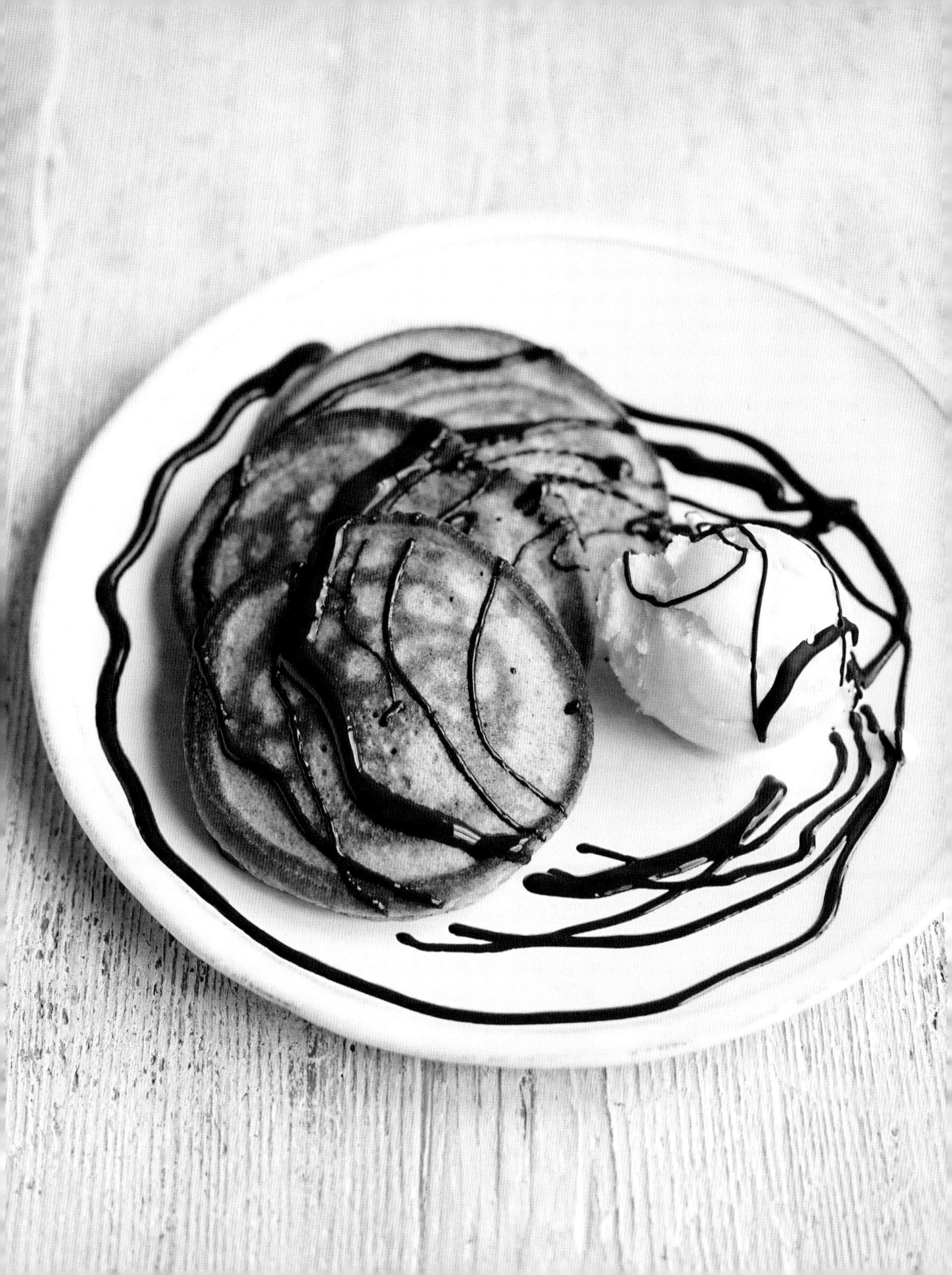

Blueberry Pancakes

Serves 4

1 cup milk

2 eggs

½ cup superfine sugar

6 tablespoons butter, melted, plus extra for greasing

1 teaspoon baking powder

pinch of salt

2 cups all-purpose flour

⅔ cup blueberries, plus extra to serve

maple syrup or honey, to serve

- Beat together the milk, eggs, sugar, and melted butter in a large bowl. Beat in the baking powder and salt, add half the flour, and beat well until all the ingredients are incorporated, then beat in the remaining flour. Stir in the blueberries to mix well.

- Heat a large, nonstick skillet over medium-high heat. Grease the bottom of the skillet with a little melted butter using paper towels. Lower the heat to medium. Spoon in large tablespoons of the batter until the skillet is full, allowing for a little space between each pancake. Add extra butter for cooking if required.

- Cook for 1–2 minutes on each side or until golden brown, then set aside and keep warm. Continue until all the batter is used.

- Divide the pancakes among 4 plates that have been warmed in a preheated oven, at 300°F, and drizzle with a little maple syrup or honey. Serve immediately, with extra blueberries.

1 Blueberry Cheesecakes

Crush 4 gingersnaps and place in the bottom of 4 individual dessert glasses. Mix together 8 oz mascarpone, ¼ cup heavy cream, ¼ cup confectioners' sugar, and the juice and grated zest of 1 lemon. Spoon over the cookie crust, top with 1 cup blueberries, and serve.

2 Brioche French Toast with Blueberry Compote

Make the compote by gently heating ⅔ cup blueberries in a saucepan with 2 tablespoons superfine sugar and a squeeze of lemon juice. When the blueberries start to burst and release their juices, simmer for 2–3 minutes, until they reach a jamlike consistency. Meanwhile, make the French toast. In a wide bowl, mix together 2 eggs, ¼ cup milk, 1 tablespoon superfine sugar, and a few drops of vanilla extract and stir until the sugar has dissolved. Dip 4 thick slices of brioche in the egg mixture to thoroughly coat. Heat a little butter in a large skillet and cook the brioche until golden brown on both sides. Serve the French toast with a scoop of vanilla ice cream and the blueberry compote.

30 French Toast with Mixed Berries

Serves 4

3 eggs
½ cup milk
¼ cup heavy cream
½ cup superfine sugar
2 teaspoons ground cinnamon
6 slices thick white bread
2¾ cups mixed berries, such
  as blueberries, raspberries,
  or red currants
2 tablespoons water
6 tablespoons butter
crème fraîche or whipped cream,
  to serve

- In a large bowl, whisk together the eggs, milk, cream, half the sugar, and a pinch of the cinnamon.

- Soak the bread in the egg mixture for a couple of minutes.

- In a skillet over medium, combine the remaining cinnamon with the remaining superfine sugar and toss the berries in the mixture until they are well coated. Add the water and heat the mixture for 3–4 minutes. Remove from the heat and keep warm.

- In a separate, large nonstick skillet, melt half the butter. Carefully drain 3 slices of bread and cook for 2–3 minutes on each side, or until golden brown. Repeat with the remaining butter and the remaining 3 slices of bread. Drain the toast on paper towels, cut each in half diagonally, and arrange the slices on serving plates that have been warmed in a preheated oven, at 300°F.

- Spoon the berry mixture around and serve immediately with a dollop of crème fraîche.

---

10 Berry and Brioche Toast
Lightly toast 4 thick slices of brioche. Whip ¼ cup heavy cream with ¼ cup superfine sugar until stiff and spread on top of the toasted brioche slices. Spoon over 1½ cups mixed blueberries and raspberries, dust with confectioners' sugar, and serve.

---

20 Crunchy Creamy Berry Sundaes
Whisk 1¾ cups heavy cream in a bowl. Coarsely break 2 meringue nests into the cream and add 1 cup raspberries and 1⅓ cups blueberries. Gently fold together so that the fruit is marbled through the cream. Place a large scoop of vanilla ice cream in the bottom of 4 sundae glasses, top with spoonfuls of the berry cream, and dust with confectioners' sugar.

 Instant Mixed Berry Sorbet

Serves 4

2 cups frozen mixed berries, such as raspberries, strawberries, and/or blueberries

2 cups raspberry yogurt

⅓ cup confectioners' sugar

- Put the frozen berries, yogurt, and sugar into a food processor or blender. Process until blended.
- Scrape the mixture from the sides and blend again.
- Spoon into chilled glasses or bowls and serve immediately.

Frozen Berries with White and Dark Hot Chocolate Sauce

Divide 3½ cups frozen mixed berries among 4 chilled serving plates or shallow bowls. Melt 4 oz semisweet dark chocolate and 4 oz white chocolate in 2 separate small saucepans. Whisk ⅔ cup heavy cream until it forms soft peaks. When ready to serve, drizzle the hot chocolate sauces over the frozen berries and serve immediately with a dollop of the whipped cream.

Miniature Mixed Berry Clafoutis

Lightly grease four 1 cup ramekins and divide 2½ cups thawed, frozen mixed berries among them. Beat ½ cup cream cheese with ¾ cup superfine sugar and ⅓ cup all-purpose flour until smooth. Beat in a few drops of vanilla extract, 3 eggs, and ⅓ cup milk. Pour evenly over the berries and bake in a preheated oven, at 400°F, for 20 minutes or until golden brown. Dust with confectioners' sugar and serve with raspberry yogurt.

Mango and Vanilla Fools

Serves 4

4 firm, ripe, sweet mangoes
1 cup canned mango puree
¼ cup superfine sugar
⅔ cup heavy cream
¼ teaspoon crushed cardamom
seeds, plus extra to decorate
1 cup store-bought vanilla
pudding or freshly prepared
instant vanilla pudding
or custard

- Peel and pit the mango and cut the flesh into small bite-size cubes. Place three-quarters of the mango into a blender along with the mango puree and sugar and blend until smooth.

- Lightly whisk the cream with the cardamom seeds until it forrms soft peaks and gently fold in the vanilla pudding. Lightly fold one-quarter of the mango mixture into the pudding mixture to create a marbled effect.

- Divide half the remaining mango cubes among 4 individual serving glasses and top with half the fool. Layer over half the remaining mango mixture.

- Decorate with the remaining mango cubes and a sprinkling of crushed cardamom seeds, then chill until ready to serve.

Mango and Cardamom Lassi

Peel and pit 3 ripe mangoes and place the flesh in a blender with ¼ cup honey, 2 cups plain yogurt, and 1 teaspoon crushed cardamom seeds. Process until smooth, pour into 4 tall, ice-filled glasses, and serve.

Fragrant Mango Tarts

Cut a sheet of ready-to-bake puff pastry in half lengthwise, then cut each half into 4 even rectangles. Place on a baking sheet lined with parchment paper. Brush with 2 tablespoons milk and sprinkle with 1 tablespoon demerara sugar or other raw sugar. Peel, pit, and thinly slice 2 ripe mangoes. Arrange the slices on the pastry rectangles, then drizzle over 2 tablespoons honey and scatter with 1 teaspoon crushed cardamom seeds. Bake in a preheated oven, at 400°F, for 15–20 minutes, until puffed up and golden. Serve with fresh whipped cream.

Berries with Meringue

Serves 4

3½ cups mixed berries (such as
blackberries, strawberries,
raspberries, and/or blueberries),
plus extra to decorate

1¾ cups strawberry yogurt

1¼ cups crème fraîche or
Greek yogurt

¼ cup confectioners' sugar

4 meringue nests, coarsely
crushed

- Place half the berries in a blender and blend until smooth.
Transfer to a bowl with the strawberry yogurt and stir to
mix well.

- Place the remaining berries in a bowl and mix in the crème
fraîche and confectioners' sugar. Add this mixture to the
berry and yogurt mixture and swirl through to create a
marbled effect.

- Fold in the crushed meringue and spoon into 4 chilled
dessert glasses.

- Serve immediately, decorated with berries.

**Layered Mixed
Berry and Yogurt
Compote** Heat 4 cups mixed
berries, such as strawberries,
raspberries, and blueberries, in
a saucepan with ¼ cup superfine
sugar and a few drops of vanilla
extract for 4–5 minutes, until
just soft and bursting. Remove
from the heat and let cool.
Spoon half the mixture into
4 dessert glasses or bowls. Top
with 1 cup strawberry yogurt,
then with the remaining berry
mixture. Scatter with 2 crumbled
meringue nests and serve at
room temperature or chilled.

**Mixed Berry
Trifles** Gently
cook 1⅓ cups each raspberries,
blueberries, and blackberries,
¼ cup superfine sugar, and
2 tablespoons water in a small
saucepan for 2–3 minutes, until
the fruits are just soft. Let cool.
Break 4–8 ladyfingers into small
pieces and use to line 4 individual
dessert bowls or glasses. Spoon
over the berry mixture followed
by 1 cup freshly prepared instant
vanilla pudding or fresh custard.
Top each with a spoonful of
crème fraîche or whipped cream
and chill until ready to serve.

30 Peach and Raspberry Cheesecake Desserts

Serves 4

5 oz mascarpone cheese
finely grated zest and juice
of 1 lemon
⅓ cup superfine sugar, plus
1 tablespoon
⅔ cup heavy cream
3 cups fresh raspberries
4 fresh ripe peaches

- Beat the mascarpone with the lemon zest and juice and sugar until smooth. Whisk the cream until it just holds its shape, then fold into the cheese mixture.

- Blend one-quarter of the raspberries in a food processor or blender with the remaining 1 tablespoon superfine sugar, for 1–2 minutes or until smooth. Transfer to a bowl. Fold in the remaining berries.

- Peel, pit, and cut the peaches into thick slices and arrange half the slices in the bottom of 4 dessert glasses or bowls.

- Spoon half the cheese mixture over the peaches and then top with the raspberry mixture. Continue to layer, finishing off with the raspberry mixture. Chill until ready to serve.

---

10 Peach and Raspberry Salad with Lemon Mascarpone

Arrange the slices from 4 ripe, peeled, and pitted peaches on a serving platter with 1⅔ cups raspberries. Whisk together 4 oz mascarpone with ⅓ cup heavy cream, the juice and finely grated zest of ½ lemon, and ¼ cup superfine sugar. Serve the fruit salad with a generous dollop of the cream mixture.

20 Peach and Raspberry Zabaglione

Place the slices from 3 ripe, peeled, and pitted peaches into a large skillet over medium-high heat and sprinkle with 2 tablespoons superfine sugar and 3 tablespoons Marsala. Cook for 2–3 minutes, until just tender. Spoon into 4 dessert glasses, top with 1 cup raspberries, and set aside. Whisk 4 egg yolks and ⅓ cup superfine sugar in a stainless steel or heatproof glass bowl for 5 minutes, until thick and pale yellow. Place the bowl over a saucepan of barely simmering water and whisk for 15 minutes, drizzling in ⅔ cup Marsala, until the mixture almost triples in volume and is light, foamy, and holding soft peaks. Be careful to avoid overheating the mixture or it will begin to cook. Spoon on top of the peaches and raspberries and serve while still warm.

Rhubarb, Orange, and Ginger Desserts

Serves 4

6 rhubarb stalks

2 pieces of preserved ginger in syrup (from a jar), drained and finely chopped

¼ cup superfine sugar

2 cloves

1 cinnamon stick

2 oranges, 1 juiced and 1 peeled and segmented

¼ cup mascarpone cheese

½ cup plain yogurt

- Cut the rhubarb into bite-size pieces and place in a saucepan with half the ginger, the sugar, cloves, cinnamon stick, and the orange juice.

- Place over high heat and when bubbling, reduce the heat, cover with a lid, and simmer, stirring occasionally, for 4–5 minutes or until just tender. Discard the cloves and cinnamon and let cool.

- Divide the orange segments among 4 dessert glasses. Beat together the mascarpone and yogurt until smooth, then layer alternately with the rhubarb and the mascarpone mixture in the glasses.

- Chill until ready to serve, topping each with the remaining chopped ginger.

1 ● Stewed Rhubarb and Ginger

Compote Place 4 cups chopped rhubarb in a saucepan with ¼ cup coarsely chopped preserved ginger, the juice and finely grated zest of 1 orange, and ½ cup superfine sugar and bring to a boil. Cook for 3–4 minutes or until the rhubarb has softened. Serve warm, spooned over scoops of vanilla ice cream.

2 ● Rhubarb and Ginger Crisps

Grease four 1¼ cup ramekins or ovenproof dishes. Place 8 rhubarb stalks chopped into 1 inch pieces into the ramekins. Add 2 tablespoons finely chopped preserved ginger with a little of the syrup from the jar and sprinkle with 1 teaspoon superfine sugar. Divide 1 cup store-bought vanilla pudding, freshly prepared instant vanilla pudding, or fresh custard among the ramekins and set aside. Rub together ¾ cup all-purpose flour with 6 tablespoons butter until the mixture resembles bread crumbs. Stir in ¼ cup superfine sugar and sprinkle over the pudding. Bake in a preheated oven, at 350°F, for 15 minutes, or until bubbling and golden.

Chocolate Fondue with a Selection of Dippers

Serves 4

12 oz dark semisweet chocolate, broken into small pieces
2 tablespoons unsalted butter
⅔ cup heavy cream
¼ cup milk
strawberries and marshmallows, for dipping

- In a small saucepan, gently heat the chocolate, butter, cream, and milk, stirring occasionally, until the chocolate is melted and the sauce is glossy and smooth. Transfer to a warm bowl or fondue pot.

- Thread 1 or 2 strawberries and marshmallows onto skewers, dip into the dark chocolate fondue, and eat immediately.

Chocolate-Dipped Strawberries

Melt 8 oz semsisweet dark chocolate in a small saucepan. Line a baking sheet with parchment paper. Dip 20 ripe strawberries into the chocolate to coat two-thirds of the way up. Place on the baking sheet and chill in the refrigerator until set and ready to serve.

Chocolate-Stuffed Croissants with

Strawberries Line a baking sheet with parchment paper. Chop an 8 oz bar of semisweet dark chocolate into small squares. Split open 4 croissants and tuck the chocolate squares inside each one. Place the croissants on the baking sheet and bake in a preheated oven, at 325°F, for 8–10 minutes or until the chocolate melts and the croissants are warm through. Dust the croissants with confectioners' sugar and serve with scoops of vanilla ice cream and strawberries.

Spiced Caramelized Pineapple with Rum

Serves 4

4 tablespoons butter
¼ cup superfine sugar
3¾ cups pineapple chunks
2–3 star anise
1 cinnamon stick
2–3 tablespoons of dark rum
cream or ice cream, to serve

- Heat the butter in a large skillet until it begins to foam.

- Add the sugar, pineapple, star anise, and cinnamon stick and cook for 5–6 minutes over high heat, stirring continuously, until the sugar mixture starts to caramelize.

- Pour in the rum and stir to mix well. Cook for another 1–2 minutes, then remove from the heat and serve immediately with a dollop of cream or ice cream.

Pineapple Kebabs with Spiced Sugar

Sprinkle Using a mortar and pestle, grind together ¼ cup superfine sugar, 1 teaspoon ground cinnamon, and 1 teaspoon crushed star anise. Thread 3 cups fresh pineapple cubes onto 8 wooden skewers. Sprinkle with the spiced sugar and serve with a dollop of cream.

Spiced Rum-Poached Pineapple

Place 3¾ cups fresh pineapple cubes into a saucepan with 1¾ cups water, ⅓ cup dark rum, 1 cinnamon stick, 2 star anise, 2 cloves, and ¾ cup superfine sugar and bring to a boil. Reduce the heat to low and cook gently for 12–15 minutes. Remove from the heat, discard the spices, and let cool. Serve warm or cold in bowls with the poaching liquid and a dollop of cream or scoop of ice cream.

30 Fresh Berry Tart

Serves 4

1 (12 oz) package puff pastry
1 cup heavy cream
⅓ cup store-bought vanilla pudding, freshly prepared instant vanilla pudding, or fresh custard
1 tablespoon kirsch or cherry liqueur
2 cups blackberries
1⅓ cups raspberries
1⅓ cups blueberries
confectioners' sugar, to dust

- On a floured surface, thinly roll out the pastry to fit a 9 inch tart pan. Trim the edges with a sharp knife and place on a baking sheet.

- Using the tip of a knife, score the pastry ¾ inch from the edge to form a border.

- Bake the pastry shell in a preheated oven, at 425°F, for 12–15 minutes or until puffed up and golden.

- Remove from the oven and press the bottom of the pastry down to create a shell with raised sides. Set aside to cool.

- Whisk the cream until stiff and then mix in the pudding or custard and kirsch or liqueur. Spoon into the center of the cooled pastry shell.

- Arrange the fruit attractively on the cream mixture, dust with confectioners' sugar, and serve immediately.

1 Mixed Berries, Kirsch, and Vanilla Desserts

Mix together 1⅓ cups each blackberries, raspberries, and blueberries in a bowl with ¼ cup superfine sugar and 2 tablespoons kirsch. Spoon into 4 deep, individual ramekins or dessert bowls. Spoon over 1¾ cups store-bought vanilla pudding, freshly prepared instant vanilla pudding, or fresh custard, dust with unsweetened cocoa powder, and serve immediately.

2 Berry and Lemon Syllabubs

Crumble 4 shortbread cookies into the bottom of 4 sundae glasses. Drizzle 1 tablespoon kirsch into each glass. Whisk 1 cup heavy cream in a bowl and add ¼ cup confectioners' sugar. Add ½ cup lemon curd or prepared instant lemon-flavored pudding and 1⅓ cups lightly crushed, mixed fresh berries and lightly fold to create a marbled effect. Spoon the cream mixture into the glasses. Top with 2 tablespoons slivered almonds and a sprig of mint and serve.

Strawberry and Cream Layer Cake

Serves 4

1 store-bought plain sponge cake
(about 16 in diameter)
⅔ cup heavy cream
8 oz small strawberries, halved
½ cup strawberry jam
confectioners' sugar, to dust

- Halve the sponge cake horizontally and place the bottom on a serving plate.

- Whip the cream until it forms soft peaks and spread over the cut side of the bottom half of the cake with a rubber spatula.

- Mix together the strawberries and jam and spoon carefully over the cream.

- Top with the sponge lid, press down lightly, and dust the top with confectioners' sugar. Cut into thick slices and serve immediately.

---

20 **Indian Strawberry Shrikhand**

Hull and coarsely chopped 10 oz strawberries and place in a bowl with 2 tablespoons rosewater and ⅓ cup confectioners' sugar. Line 4 dessert bowls with a thick slice of sponge cake and spoon the strawberry mixture on top. Beat together 1⅔ cups thick Greek yogurt with ½ cup strawberry jam and spoon over the strawberry mixture. Chill until ready to serve.

30 **Miniature Layer Cakes** Grease and line the bottom of 8 individual, springform cake pans (about 4 inches diameter) and put on a baking sheet. Beat ¼ lb plus 2 tablespoons (1¼ sticks) butter with ¾ cup superfine sugar in a bowl until pale and fluffy. In a separate bowl, beat 3 eggs with a few drops of vanilla extract, and gradually beat into the butter mixture. Sift 1¼ cups all-purpose flour with 1¾ teaspoons baking powder over the mixture and

gently fold in until just combined. Divide evenly among the prepared cake pans, smoothing the surface. Bake in a preheated oven, at 350°F, for 20 minutes or until risen and golden. Cool in the pans, then turn out onto a wire rack and cool. Meanwhile, lightly whip 1¼ cups heavy cream to form soft peaks and spread over 4 of the cooled sponges. Top with 2 tablespoons strawberry jam and sandwich with the remaining sponges. Dust each with confectioners' sugar to serve.

 Tropical Fruit Trifles

Serves 4

1 large passionfruit
2 tablespoons confectioners'
    sugar (or to taste)
juice of 1 orange
4 kiwis
1 mango
10–12 seedless green and
    red grapes
4 thick slices sponge cake
1¾ cups store-bought vanilla
    pudding, freshly prepared
    instant vanilla pudding, or
    fresh custard

For the topping

½ cup heavy cream, softly
    whipped
julienned orange zest,
    to decorate

- Prepare the fruit by scraping the seeds from a passionfruit into a large mixing bowl. Mix in the confectioners' sugar and orange juice.

- Peel and finely dice the kiwis. Peel the mango, then cut the flesh into ½ inch dice.

- Add the diced fruit to the passionfruit mixture with the grapes. Chill until ready to serve.

- To assemble the trifles, take 4 dessert bowls or glasses and arrange the cake and fruit salad in the bottom. Pour the vanilla pudding over the top.

- Place a dollop of whipped cream on top of the pudding and serve decorated with the orange zest.

---

1 **Tropical Fruit Salad**
Place 1 cubed mango in a bowl with 2 cups pineapple chunks, 4 peeled and cubed kiwis, and 1⅓ cups seedless green and red grapes. Add the juice of 1 orange and ⅓ cup confectioners' sugar and toss to mix well. Serve with ice cream.

2 **Tropical Fruit and Vanilla Tart**
Line the bottom of an 8 inch store-bought pastry shell with 1 cup store-bought vanilla pudding or freshly prepared instant vanilla pudding. Peel, halve, and pit 2 ripe mangoes and cut into thin slices. Peel 2 kiwis and cut into thin slices. Arrange the mango and kiwi slices over the pudding in the pastry shell with ⅔ cup halved green and red seedless grapes. Dust with confectioners' sugar and serve with whipped cream.

VEG-DESS-VYH

Watermelon, Lime, and Grenadine Squares

Serves 4

¼ cup grenadine
¼ cup superfine sugar
juice and finely grated zest
  of 1 lime, plus extra lime zest
  to decorate
½ cup water
1 small watermelon

- Place the grenadine, sugar, and lime juice and zest with the measured water in a small saucepan and bring to a boil. Reduce the heat and cook gently for 6–8 minutes, until thick and syrupy. Remove from the heat and let cool.

- Meanwhile halve the watermelon and, using a sharp knife, slice the rind from the bottom of each half.

- Lay the halves on a cutting board and, working from top to bottom, trim the rind from the watermelon flesh in 4 cuts, creating 2 large squares.

- Cut each square of watermelon into equal bite-size squares and place on a serving platter to form a neat large square (made up of the bite-size squares).

- Drizzle over the cooled grenadine syrup, scatter with the lime zest, and serve immediately.

10 Iced Watermelon, Lime, and Grenadine Coolers Process the flesh of ½ watermelon in a blender with ¼ cup grenadine, ¼ cup superfine sugar, ¼ cup chopped mint, and the juice and finely grated zest of 1 lime. Fill 4 tall glasses with crushed ice, pour over the watermelon mixture, and serve immediately.

30 Watermelon Kebabs with Lime and Mint Syrup Heat 1 cup superfine sugar in a saucepan with ⅔ cup water and bring to a boil. Reduce the heat and cook gently for 15–20 minutes, until the sugar has dissolved and the mixture has thickened. Remove from the heat and stir in the juice and finely grated zest of 1 lime and ¼ cup finely chopped mint. Let cool. Meanwhile, cut the flesh from ½ watermelon into bite-size cubes and thread onto 8 wooden skewers. Place on a shallow platter and pour the lime syrup over them. Serve at room temperature or chilled.

20 Blackberry, Cinnamon, and Apple Cranachan

Serves 4

4 teaspoons rolled oats
3 tablespoons superfine sugar
1 cup vanilla yogurt
½ teaspoon ground cinnamon
1 tablespoon whiskey
3 cups blackberries,
    plus extra for decoration
2 tablespoons butter
1 apple, such as Pink Lady
    or Fuji, peeled, cored, and
    coarsely grated

- Place a small skillet over medium high heat. Add the oats and cook for 1 minute, then add 1 tablepoon of the sugar.

- Dry-fry, stirring for 2–3 minutes, or until the oats are lightly browned, then transfer to a piece of nonstick parchment paper and let cool. Mix together the yogurt, cinnamon, 1 teaspoon of the sugar, and the whiskey.

- Stir in the blackberries, crushing them slightly.

- Heat a nonstick saucepan over high heat, add the butter, and sauté the apple for 3–4 minutes. When the apple begins to soften, add the remaining sugar and cook until lightly browned. Set aside to cool.

- Layer the blackberry mixture with the apple in 4 dessert glasses. Top with blackberries, sprinkle the oat mixture on top, and serve.

10 Warm Blackberry and Cinnamon

Compote Heat 4 cups blackberries with 1 teaspoon ground cinnamon, ¼ cup superfine sugar, and a squeeze of lemon juice in a saucepan and bring to a boil. Cook for 5–6 minutes or until the berries have broken down and the mixture has thickened. Serve warm over scoops of ice cream or with vanilla yogurt.

30 Individual Crunchy Blackberry and

Apple Crisps Peel, core, and chop 1¼ lb Granny Smith apples into small chunks. Squeeze the juice of ½ lemon over the apple chunks and mix well. In four 1¼ cup ramekins or ovenproof dishes, layer the apples with 1⅓ cups blackberries and 1 cup demerara or other raw sugar. For the crumble topping, rub ½ lb (2 sticks) butter into 2 cups all-purpose flour in a large bowl until the mixture resembles bread crumbs. Mix in 1½ cups muesli and ¼ cup firmly packed brown sugar and stir. Sprinkle the crumble topping evenly over the fruit. Bake in a preheated oven, at 400°F, for 20 minutes or until the fruit is cooked and bubbling juices seep through the topping. Cool for a few minutes and then serve with fresh cream.

Chocolate and Raspberry Roulade

Serves 4

butter, for greasing

4 oz semisweet dark chocolate, broken into squares

4 extra-large eggs, separated

½ cup superfine sugar

⅓ cup all-purpose flour, sifted

½ teaspoon baking powder

1¼ cups heavy cream

2½ cups raspberries, plus extra to decorate

unsweetened cocoa powder, for dusting

- Grease and line a 12 x 9 inch jelly roll pan with nonstick parchment paper.

- Melt the chocolate in a heatproof bowl over a saucepan of barely simmering water.

- In a large bowl, beat the egg yolks and sugar until pale and creamy. Stir in the chocolate, flour, and baking powder.

- Using a clean whisk or beaters, beat the egg whites in a separate bowl until stiff peaks form. Carefully fold the whites into the chocolate mixture until well combined.

- Transfer the batter to the prepared pan and shake to level it. Bake in a preheated oven, at 350°F, for 15–20 minutes, or until the sponge is slightly risen and just firm to the touch.

- Carefully invert the sponge onto nonstick parchment paper. Peel the paper from the bottom of the roulade and discard. Roll up in the fresh paper.

- Whip the cream and gently fold in the raspberries.

- Unroll the roulade and spread over the raspberry cream, leaving a small gap around the edge. Reroll the roulade (don't worry about any cracks). Dust with the cocoa powder, decorate with raspberries, and serve immediately.

---

1 Chocolate and Raspberry Squares

Whip ¼ cup cream and spread over 4 store-bought chocolate brownies. Top each with 10–12 raspberries, dust with confectioners' sugar, and serve immediately.

2 Melting Chocolate Soufflés with Raspberries

Raspberries Grease 4 medium ramekins. Melt 8 oz semisweet dark chocolate with ¼ lb plus 2 tablespoons (1¼ sticks) butter in a bowl over simmering water or in a microwave. Beat 4 eggs with ¾ cup superfine sugar until light and fluffy, then sift in

¾ cup all-purpose flour. Fold in the chocolate mixture. Divide among the ramekins and bake in a preheated oven, at 350°F, for 8–12 minutes. The soufflés should rise and form a firm crust but should still be slightly runny in the middle. Serve each with a handful of raspberries and cream.

30 Lime, Banana, and Coconut Fritters

Serves 4

juice of 2 limes
⅓ cup superfine sugar
4 bananas, sliced into three
  or four pieces
1⅔ cups cornstarch
¾ cup all-purpose flour
1 teaspoon baking powder
3 tablespoons dried shredded
  coconut
3 extra-large egg yolks
⅓ cup chilled soda or sparkling
  water
vegetable oil, for deep-frying
confectioners' sugar, for dusting
honey, for drizzling

- Mix together the lime juice and superfine sugar in a bowl. Add the bananas, stir well to coat, and let stand for 5 minutes.

- Roll the bananas in half the cornstarch until well coated and set aside. Sift the remaining cornstarch, flour, and baking powder into a bowl. Add the coconut.

- Beat together the egg yolks and soda or sparkling water in a clean bowl. Add the flour mixture and beat again until the mixture forms a thick batter.

- Fill a deep, medium saucepan one-quarter full of vegetable oil. Heat the oil to 350°F or until a cube of bread turns golden in 10–15 seconds.

- Dip the bananas into the batter and carefully place into the hot vegetable oil to deep-fry for 1–2 minutes, in batches, until golden brown. Carefully remove with a slotted spoon and drain on paper towels. Keep warm on a plate in a preheated oven, at 300°F.

- Serve immediately, dusted with confectioners' sugar and drizzled with honey.

10 Boozy Strawberries with Lime and Coconut

In a large bowl, mix together 2 tablespoons superfine sugar, 2 tablespoons Cointreau or orange liqueur, and the juice of ½ lime. Stir in 2½ cups freshly shredded coconut and 1¼ cups chopped strawberries. Toss to mix well and serve.

20 Lime and Coconut Rice Pudding

Heat 1 cup half-and-half and ½ cup coconut milk in a saucepan with ¾ cup superfine sugar, ¼ teaspoon vanilla extract, and the finely grated zest of 2 limes. Bring to a boil and add 1⅔ cups cold, cooked rice. Cook for 4–5 minutes, until thickened. Ladle into bowls and serve decorated with mint sprigs.

Individual Mixed Berry Swirl Cheesecakes

Serves 4

2 tablespoons butter
1 tablespoon light corn syrup
4 oz chocolate cookies

For the filling

1¾ cups mixed berries, such
  as raspberries, blackberries,
  and blueberries, plus extra
  to decorate
¾ cup cream cheese
½ cup superfine sugar
juice and grated zest of 1 lemon
½ teaspoon vanilla extract
2 tablespoons water
½ envelope gelatin
1 cup heavy cream
mint, to decorate

- Place the butter and corn syrup in a saucepan and melt over medium heat. Process the cookies into crumbs in a food processor (or bash with a rolling pin in a plastic bag) and add to the pan.

- Puree the berries in a food processor or blender (or rub through a strainer), then strain to remove the seeds; set aside.

- Line a baking sheet with nonstick parchment paper and divide the cookie mixture among four 4 inch molds, pressing down well. Chill until needed.

- To make the filling, beat together the cream cheese, sugar, lemon zest and juice, and vanilla extract. Sprinkle the gelatin into the measured water in a small bowl and microwave on high for 30 seconds. Mix a little of the cheese mixture into the gelatin, then stir the gelatin back into the cheese mixture.

- Meanwhile, beat the cream to form soft peaks, fold into the cheese mixture with the berry puree, and swirl gently to create a marbled effect. Pour into the molds and flatten with a rubber spatula. Chill until ready to serve.

- To serve, release the cakes from the molds by running a knife around the edge. Decorate with berries and mint.

10 Boozy Chocolate and Berry Desserts

Melt 4 oz semisweet dark chocolate in a saucepan and stir in 1 cup fresh mixed berries. In a bowl, beat 1 cup cream cheese with 3 tablespoons brandy and 2 tablespoons superfine sugar. Spoon the chocolate mixture into the bottom of 4 dessert bowls and top with the cream cheese mixture. Serve chilled or at room temperature.

20 Mini Berry Cheesecake

Pavlovas Beat together 1 cup cream cheese with ⅓ cup confectioners' sugar and a few drops of vanilla extract. Stir 2½ cups fresh mixed berries into the cream cheese mixture and divide among 8 meringue nests. Melt 2 oz semisweet dark chocolate in a small saucepan and drizzle it over the pavlovas. Serve immediately.

VEG-DESS-WAT

Mango and Mint Carpaccio

Serves 4

⅓ cup superfine sugar

finely grated zest and juice
   of 1 large lime

2 tablespoons finely chopped
   mint, plus extra leaves
   to decorate

⅓–½ cup water

4 firm, ripe mangoes

vanilla ice cream, to serve
   (optional)

- Put the sugar in a small saucepan with the lime zest and juice, mint, and measured water. Bring to a boil and remove from the heat. Stir until the sugar is dissolved. Set aside to cool.

- Meanwhile, cut the mangoes in half, running a sharp knife around the pits to detach them. Peel and slice the flesh as thinly as possible.

- Arrange the mango slices on 4 serving plates and drizzle with the sugar syrup.

- Serve with vanilla ice cream, if desired, and decorate with mint leaves.

Hot Toffee Mangoes with Lime

Heat a skillet over medium heat and cook ⅓ cup superfine sugar until it starts to melt and turn golden. Add 4 tablespoons butter and 2 peeled, pitted, and thickly sliced mangoes and cook for 5–6 minutes or until the mango is coated in the sugar syrup. Add the finely grated zest and juice of 1 lime, then simmer for 2 minutes. Serve hot with a sprinkling of chopped mint and vanilla ice cream.

Grilled Mango with Lime and Mint

Syrup Slowly melt 1 cup superfine sugar in a saucepan over medium heat until dark amber. Remove from the heat and carefully add ½ cup lime juice and ¼ cup finely chopped mint. Return to the heat and stir until the caramel melts again. Cool and set aside until needed. Beat 8 oz mascarpone, ⅔ cup half-and-half, 3 tablespoons confectioners' sugar, and ¼ teaspoon vanilla extract together until smooth. Chill until required. Cut 4 ripe mangoes into "mango cheeks": hold the mango vertically and, using a sharp knife, cut down both sides of the pit. Sprinkle 2 tablespoons superfine sugar onto the cut side of the mango cheeks, shaking off any excess. Grill on a nonstick grill pan, cut side down, for 4–5 minutes. Arrange the mango cheeks on a plate, grilled side up. Serve with the coconut cream mixture and drizzle the syrup over the top.

VEG-DESS-XOF

Index

Page references in *italics* indicate photographs.

Acknowledgments

Executive editor: Eleanor Maxfield
Senior editor: Leanne Bryan
Copy-editor: Nikki Sims
Art director: Jonathan Christie
Design concept and layout: www.gradedesign.com
Art editors: Juliette Norsworthy & Mark Kan
Photographer: Will Heap
Home economist: Sunil Vijayakar
Stylist: Isabel De Cordova
Production manager: Katherine Hockley